# FAITH AND STRUGGLE IN THE LIVES OF FOUR AFRICAN AMERICANS

ALSO AVAILABLE FROM BLOOMSBURY

*The African Christian Diaspora*, Afe Adogame
*Catholic Culture in the USA*, John Portmann
*The Collected Writings of Charles H. Long*, edited by Charles H. Long
*The Spiritual Virtuoso*, Marion Goldman and Steven Pfaff

# FAITH AND STRUGGLE IN THE LIVES OF FOUR AFRICAN AMERICANS

*Ethel Waters, Mary Lou Williams, Eldridge Cleaver, and Muhammad Ali*

RANDAL MAURICE JELKS

BLOOMSBURY ACADEMIC
LONDON • NEW YORK • OXFORD • NEW DELHI • SYDNEY

BLOOMSBURY ACADEMIC
Bloomsbury Publishing Plc
50 Bedford Square, London, WC1B 3DP, UK
1385 Broadway, New York, NY 10018, USA

BLOOMSBURY, BLOOMSBURY ACADEMIC and the Diana logo are trademarks of
Bloomsbury Publishing Plc

First published in Great Britain 2019

Library of Congress Cataloging-in-Publication Data
Names: Jelks, Randal Maurice, 1956- author.
Title: Faith and struggle in the lives of four African Americans : Ethel Waters,
Mary Lou Williams, Eldridge Cleaver and Muhammad Ali / Randal
Maurice Jelks.
Description: New York, NY : Bloomsbury Academic, 2019. | Includes bibliographical
references and index.
Identifiers: LCCN 2018030756 | ISBN 9781350074620 (pbk.)
Subjects: LCSH: African Americans–Religious life. | Waters, Ethel, 1896-1977–Religion. |
Williams, Mary Lou, 1910-1981–Religion. | Ali, Muhammad, 1942-2016–Religion. |
Cleaver, Eldridge, 1935-1998–Religion.
Classification: LCC BL625.2 .J45 2019 | DDC 200.8996073–dc23 LC record available at
https://lccn.loc.gov/2018030756

ISBN: HB: 978-1-3500-7461-3
PB: 978-1-3500-7462-0
ePDF: 978-1-3500-7464-4
eBook: 978-1-3500-7463-7

Typeset by Deanta Global Publishing Services, Chennai, India
Printed and bound in Great Britain

*Dedicated to my Father, Brother, Uncle, and Friends*

*Hebrews 11:39–40 (NRSV)*

Yet all these, though they were commended for their faith, did not receive what was promised, since God had provided something better so that they would not, apart from us, be made perfect.

*Felix Armfield (August 27, 1962–April 30, 2014)*
*William Henry Dungey, Jr. (October 20, 1963–March 17, 2014)*
*Thomas Jackson (December 24, 1938–February 1, 2015)*
*James W. Myles (May 4, 1937–October 13, 2012)*
*Julian Osibee Jelks (May 16, 1930–June 18, 2013)*
*Kevin Daniel Jelks (July 12, 1963–April 27, 2015)*
*John Allen Johnson (March 5, 1950–July 2, 2015)*
*Tyrone Perry, I. (May 23, 1956–November 27, 2014)*
*Harry "Buster" Porter (October 30, 1930–April 14, 2013)*
*Geoffrey Aaron Powell (July 9, 1983–February 14, 2013)*
*Reverend John Albert Shyne, Sr. (April 1, 1925–December 19, 2017)*

# CONTENTS

# ACKNOWLEDGMENTS

A book is an accumulated debt. My deepest gratitude goes to Bloomsbury acquisition editor Lalle Pursglove for being willing to take a chance on this book. Thanks are also due to the anonymous readers who read the initial draft of this book and gave me inestimable feedback. Gratitude also to my colleagues at the University of Kansas in the departments of African and African American Studies and American Studies. I also want to acknowledge the university's Hall Humanities Center, where I first presented my ideas regarding this book. Special thanks to my colleague Sarah Lynn Reece-Hardy for engaging me in a terrifically encouraging conversation about the subject of this book. My gratitude to Udo Hebel and the American Studies department of Regensburg University in Germany for allowing me to test my ideas on them regarding American religious pluralism. Thanks also to Masaryk University Faculty of Social Sciences and American Studies department in the Czech Republic for hosting me over the course of a wonderful Fulbright semester in an invaluable intellectual exchange. Thanks also go to Eric Michael Washington and Kristin Kobes Du Mez of Calvin College who invited me to present my ideas about this book. I cannot recall the audience member at that lecture who urged that I write my own sojourn into this book, but nevertheless hearty thanks. Thanks also goes to Michelle Nickerson who graciously invited me to Loyola University, Chicago, to discuss this work in the Ramonat Seminar in American Catholic History. My gratitude also goes to Diane Proctor Reeder, my college classmate (Go Blue!) and friend for life, an author in her own right, who served as my editorial eyes and an interlocutor on this book. Thanks is also due to Pam LeRow, a wonderful KU staff person who patiently assisted me in formatting and indexing. Additionally, thanks is owed for collegiality, friendship, and intellectual exchange—Kerri Allen North, Tony Bolden,

Tommy J. Curry, Dennis Dickerson, Ayesha Hardison, Paul Harvey, Maryemma Graham, Jennifer Hamer, Clarence Lang, Ula Yvette Taylor, John Edgar Tidwell, and Judith Wiesenfeld. Thanks also goes to journalist Jonathan Eig, a Muhammad Ali biographer, who shared with me conversation and his research on Ali. Lastly, but never least, I thank my family and friends for a steady diet of love, laughter, and tears as we support one another over the good, the bad, and the ugly or as the Negro Spiritual, *I Want Jesus to Walk with Me*, puts it "all along my pilgrim journey."

# Introduction:

# "We have been believers": Toward an inner history of African Americans

*Neither the slaves' whip nor the lynchers' rope nor the bayonet could kill our black belief.*

MARGARET WALKER[1]

I grew up a believer and I believe still. And in a nod to Margaret Walker's quote, my faith journey has had whips and ropes and bayonets along the way. Faith is neither easy nor simplistic. Being a believer can be contradictory and bewildering. It does not prevent human lamentations—drama, suffering, illness, unrequited loves and desires, or unhappiness. It does not make one qualitatively better than a nonbeliever, agnostic, or atheist. Believers have good lives and failed lives. The human datum is we are mortal; we have a limited shelf life.

Growing up as a believer has served me well. My faith communities grounded me in ethical thinking and taught me introspection, a self-awareness that pushed me to continuously examine my own shortcomings. As a believer, I constantly have to face my own heart of darkness and shed claims to innocence or moral superiority. As a believer, I frequently realize my motives are not pure whether justified by faith or no faith. And I have come to recognize that being a believer can be easily manipulated to justify political power, greed, and vanities. As a believer, I developed a sense of responsibility for others and the world around me. Belief has compelled me to give up myself in every way to build institutions from churches to hospitals to schools, and join and wage struggles for justice.

Here it is up front, a confession of my own belief. I grew up believing and for whatever reasons—psychological comfort, sunny optimism, fear of death, inspiring strength—this wellspring of hope has stuck with me and fed my intellect, forcing existential questions that define our common humanity and my personhood. As there are a myriad of human beings, there are myriad of faith journeys. We all have a story to tell.

In this regard, I cannot help but recollect the song "Blessed Assurance" whose lyrics were penned by Fanny Crosby in 1873 and became a standard among American Protestants. The song was passed on to me via vacation bible school at Greater St. Stephens Baptist Church in New Orleans, at the time a modest congregation led by Reverend Royal. I can still recollect the vigor with which we VBS kids sang Crosby's infectious refrain.

> This is my *story*, this is my song
> Praising my Savior all the day long
> This is my *story*, this is my song
> Praising my Savior all the day long (emphasis mine)

Crosby understood that faith was a narrative journey, one that we take with us everywhere we go. She framed her lyrics around a particular kind of journey of Christian faith that some will agree with and others will not. Nevertheless, her insight holds true; we all have a story!

Collectively, our stories combine to make histories. We know many of these historical narratives, read them in history books, learn them in school. Yet, these individual, personal narratives are absolutely necessary to understand what those histories mean and how they relate to the larger story of humanity.

Some of the most riveting historical narratives are those that relate to Black American experience. We know the outlines of that experience with the large narratives of enslavement, emancipation, Jim Crow, the civil rights movement, and Black Lives Matter. But my argument in these pages is that *individual* Black American stories in particular provide luminous and revealing inner histories, and they are just as important to explore as the histories of human rights protests and political activism. Inner histories reflect a solitary wrestling for individuation and the collective efforts to institutionalize civic freedoms under a variety of historical conditions.

Religious studies scholar Robert Orsi makes this argument vis-à-vis the story of American immigration. The Italian Catholic immigrant voice reveals an inner history, an analysis that is glaringly missing from histories of American immigration. Orsi writes, "Immigration was as much a spiritual event as it was a political and social response to particular historical conditions; the outward journeying was matched by a changing inner terrain."[2] Orsi's argument continues to make a great deal of sense.

The inner history of African Americans is a rich and elastic American tradition, dating back to the founding of the United States. The inventiveness of slave and spiritual narratives in the nineteenth century was as much about the freedom of the self as it was decrying the brutalities of chattel slavery. So, the argument here is that the inner history of Black lives in the twentieth century is a story worth telling. These are the introspective reflections stemming from linkages to religious communities and rituals, as well as those that are derived from disenchantment, agnosticism, or atheism. They reflect the changing landscapes of the self and the material factors that shape self-awareness.

St. Augustine, the great North African fourth-century bishop, wrote *The Confession of St. Augustine* to make theological sense of his youthful rebelliousness and his curious intellectual forays into the Roman Empire. In *Confession* Augustine distinguishes his life as a Christian convert as well as a leader of the faithful who were living on the periphery of imperious Roman rule. His thirteen-book series is at once a documentation of his personal pilgrimage and a treatise on basic tenets of Christianity with an evangelical bent. Augustine could have not ever anticipated that his introspective spiritual journey would become a template for letters written by Black America, many of whose members consider his master work an autobiographical inheritance for the despised, stigmatized, and exploited lives of American slaves. In a way, Black Americans are Augustine's North American descendants.

Of course, this analogy can bend only so far across time and space. Black American introspection was in large part not a Platonic or neo-Platonic read of Christianity as was Augustine's work. It was a read of Christianity on Black American terms, which were marked by myriad struggles with the Protestant Bible, in part due to the European Reformation[3] and in part due to the Black American propensity to interpret verses in a way that went against prevailing cultural norms.

More than a millennium later, slave narratives, elicited by from Works Progress Administration workers who had been hired for the very purpose of interviewing ex-slaves, echoed Augustine's soul-searching. Furthermore, the religious content of slave narratives is all by itself a portfolio of the American encounter with evangelical theology. The religious self-introspection abounded and continues.[4]

The abolitionist theologian Theodore Parker found something deeply profound about the literary formulas of slave narratives, something more profound than the traditional American mid-nineteenth-century novel. Parker backhandedly offered praise to the American slave narrative for its originality stating,

There is one portion of our permanent literature, if literature it may be called, which is wholly independent and original. . . . So we have one series of literary productions that could be written by none but Americans, and only here; I mean the lives of the Fugitive Slaves. But as these are not the work of men of superior culture, they hardly help to pay the scholar's debt. Yet all the original romance of Americans is in them, not in the white man's novel.[5]

Parker did not fully understand the life of bondage; he was too caught up in a culturally arrogant society to appreciate the struggles of the dispossessed. He, however, understood enough to grasp their originality within American literature. They were interior narratives of freedoms whose aim was to subvert national racism. Philosophically and theologically they mused on the meaning of individual life and death, as well as politics and society.[6]

Inner histories have been crucial expressions of Black American survival and aspiration. These self-reflections were journey of the self or selves trying to make sense of dislocation by storying. As described by the poet and literary critic Kevin Young, "storying" is the literary tradition of the self-invention and recreation in poetry, prose, fiction, and music. Young derives the idea of storying from Zora Neale Hurston's collection *Mules and Men*. Storying means the "lies" Black folk tell to amuse themselves and to explain their origins. But he makes a distinction regarding "storying" in that it is not a falsehood. According to Young, "Storying . . . counters the ongoing, reflexive desire in our culture for 'realness' in all its forms."[7] Storying, as Young discerns, are the "ways in which black folk use fiction in its various forms to free themselves from the bound fact." In other words, African Americans use storying to challenge the kind of facts or empiricism that infantilize or make them appear at best as one-dimensional figures or at worst as more pathological than other communities in America. From the perspective of an inner history, Young's idea can be expanded further. Telling the story, as Black church folk promote in a call-and-response manner to sermons, is about what one's own story means in terms of self-regard and how that story thrives and grows within communities of faith.

Though too often ignored, "storying" is a deeply philosophical search or faith quest for meaning of one's self and what it means to live collectively in an American-style democracy. This "storying" has presented what it means to be a person under conditions of brutal slave migration, the auction block, a continuous legacy of hostile socioeconomic conditions, state, and extralegal violence, and the ever-changing, perhaps global, forms of anti-Black racism, and is a remarkable tradition that often gets the short shrift.

In 1945, the theologian and mystic, Howard Thurman, published two slender volumes titled *Deep River: Reflections on the Religious Insight of Certain of the Negro Spirituals* and *The Negro Spiritual Speaks of Life and Death*. In both volumes Thurman looked back, examining slave spirituals for a greater existential significance in the atomic age. He thought that the inner lives of his slave ancestors and their collective musical composition spoke to the perennial questions of the meaning of life and death facing African Americans in his era. Slaves, Thurman contended, "discovered that which religion insists is the ultimate truth about human life and destiny. It is the supreme validation of the human spirit." This type of knowledge, he stated, "is able to transcend the vicissitudes of life, however terrifying, and look on the world with quiet eyes."[8] Thurman was remarkable; he found just as much existential wisdom in the past lives of African Americans as his contemporary, the French existential philosopher, Jean-Paul Sartre, found in French thought in his 1943 publication of *Being and Nothingness: An Essay on Phenomenological Ontology*. Thurman's slender volume also built on insights of W. E. B. DuBois, the first Harvard Black PhD, a historian, sociologist, and founding member of the National Association for the Advancement of Colored People. DuBois wrote *Souls of Black Folk*, published in 1903. In *Souls*, he examined what he called the "sorrow songs." These songs were placed in opposition to the crass commercialism of minstrelsy that dominated entertainment and Black entertainers themselves. He beautifully penned the following:

> Little of beauty has America given the world save the rude grandeur God himself stamped on her bosom; the human spirit in this new world has expressed itself in vigor and ingenuity rather than in beauty. And so, by fateful

chance the Negro folk-song—the rhythmic cry of the slave—stands to-day not simply as the sole American music, but as the most beautiful expression of human experience born this side the seas. It has been neglected, it has been, and is, half despised, and above all it has been persistently mistaken and misunderstood; but notwithstanding, it still remains as the singular spiritual heritage of the nation and the greatest gift of the Negro people.[9]

It was DuBois's insight that Thurman built upon in thinking about what Black life meant as the Second World War was coming to a close. One of Thurman's great contributions as a writer and thinker was to acknowledge that Black struggle in its contemporary manifestation required some introspective resolve about the meaningfulness of the self. More importantly to him, looking backward was really a way of thinking forward and anticipating the struggle for human rights that was ensuing globally. Presciently he noted, building off his analysis of the spirituals:

At the moment, we stand as the graphic masters of much of the earth by virtue of our vast resourcefulness, our material resources, and the techniques by which we have reduced great conglomerates of nature to simple units of control and utility. It is a terrifying truth that life is its own restraint, and the moral law that binds in judgment the life of the individual binds the nation and the race. Unless there is a great rebirth of high and holy moral courage, which will place at the center of our vast power an abiding sense of moral responsibility, both because of our treatment of minorities at home and our arrogance abroad, we may very easily become the most hated nation on earth. No amount of power, wealth, or prestige can stay this judgment. If we would be beloved we must share that kind of spirit as the expression of the true genius of our democratic government.[10]

Thurman further observed that what was important about the inner experiences of slaves is that they held a realistic hope born out of gloomy circumstances. Slaves, he suggests, shared "an elemental vigor that expressed itself in a deep optimism arising out of the pessimism of life."[11] Thurman viewed the history of America through a lens of faith, a lens he ascribed to the slave community. For him, slaves saw their lives as multidimensional. As a result, they never fully lost hope and kept dreams alive. "We continue to hope against all evidence to the contrary," he noted "because that hope is fed by a conviction deeper than the processes of thought that the destiny of man is good." This inherent goodness of life was the essence "captured by the spiritual."[12]

If there is a critique to be made of Thurman, it is his valorization of the inner life of slaves over his contemporaries. Yes, slaves offered a dimension to self-understanding and self-regard through their spiritual storying, but so did Thurman's Black contemporaries. The narration of perennial questions had not disappeared. The Second World War and the years that followed did not shrink or dissipate the inner journeys of Black Americans. A diversity of Black essayists, poets, and novelists, including Langston Hughes's poetry and his often forgotten 1930 novel *Not Without Laughter* as well as his 1940 memoir *The Big Sea*, explored the struggle for both the inward and outward dimension of freedom. Richard Wright's journey in *Black Boy* published in 1945 narrated the experiences of being a Black southerner without ties to faith or religion. Margaret Walker's tremendous book of poetry titled *For My People*, which won the Yale Series of Younger Poets Award in 1942, meditated on the inner dimensions of Black Americans from the era of slavery to contemporary Black life. No student of poetry should forget her rhythmic stanzas rendered in chanted sermonic blues rhythm:

> For my people blundering and groping and floundering in the dark of churches and schools and clubs and societies, associations and councils and committees and conventions, distressed and disturbed and deceived and devoured by money-hungry glory-craving leeches, preyed on by facile force of state and fad and novelty, by false prophet and holy believer; . . . Let a new earth rise. Let another world be born. Let a bloody peace be written in the sky. . . . Let a race of men now rise and take control.[13]

Telling the story did not end with the slave narratives. Despite the dissipation of physical enslavement that ended de jure in 1865, the need for "storying" continued among Black Americans. They storied even when they were not singing spirituals. They storied absent the assignation of great literary status. Soldiering on, they continued the rich literary tradition of writing to describe their journeys.[14] They also storied musically, as any Black southern migrant would have testified heading north or west through blues, gospel, jazz, jailhouse, jug, and minstrel. Certainly, Thurman had to have heard the "Mother of Gospel" Sallie Martin and her singers sing *Just a Closer Walk with Thee*

> I am weak, but thou art strong;
>
> Jesus, keep me from all wrong;
>
> I'll be satisfied as long
>
> as I walk, let me walk close to thee.
>
> Just a closer walk with thee,
>
> grant it, Jesus, is my plea,
>
> daily walking close to thee:
>
> Let it be, dear Lord, let it be.

Surely, as a baptist minister, Thurman heard Martin's gospel music compatriot Thomas Dorsey's lamentation *Precious Lord* and how it spoke to the existential crisis of migrating to Chicago or Detroit or Los Angeles or Oakland.[15] These contemporary storytellers do not show up in his analysis.

Here I am not critiquing Thurman for what he omitted from his daring theological/sociological observations. He offers a different voice from his contemporaries and his voice should be read in tandem with those widely known literary figures. In fact, his assessment, along with DuBois's, factored into the slave historiographies of 1970s, including John Blassingame's 1972 *The Slave Community: Plantation Life in the Antebellum South*; Eugene Genovese's 1976 *Roll, Jordan, Roll: The World the Slaves Made*; Lawrence Levine's 1977 *Black Culture and Black Consciousness: Afro-American Folk Thought from Slavery to*

*Freedom*; and Albert Raboteau's 1978 *Slave Religion: The Invisible Institution in the Antebellum South*. Thurman's spiritual readings of slavery shaped his and others' histories deeply. The power of Thurman's search for an inner meaning, a meaning he concluded was necessary for fueling contemporary democratic struggle, had an extensive reach that is often not acknowledged today. His insights influenced religious leaders, civil rights struggles, and American academicians. His work serves as reminder that spiritualized, if not romanticized, accounts of slavery were equally important as any empirical dissections of American slave histories.

Although as wonderfully mystical, appealing, and powerful as Thurman's insights are, he missed assisting his readers in describing what these inner histories meant in the moment. Contemporaneously in his era were stories of struggles for both inner and material freedoms that were being narrated collectively in fiction, essays, and memoirs. The lived religious experience of Black Americans had never halted. In fact, Black American religion and anti-religiosity was modernizing, ever adapting to historical circumstances, and evolving from the long and brutal history of slavery as an American institution. Black Americans continued to "story" about their inner journeys as did their slave forbearers.

There can be no greater ode to Black inner history than when in 1972 the recording artist Aretha Franklin, the Queen of Soul, made her magnum opus gospel album *Amazing Grace*.[16] Whether a person of faith or not, everyone in the Black community understood the inner meaning when she sang her version of Reverend William Hebert Brewster's gospel blues composition "How I Got Over."[17]

How I got over
How did I make it over
You know my soul look back and wonder
How did I make it over
How I made it over

Going on over all these years

You know my soul look back and wonder

How did I make it over.[18]

The inward lives of Black people, whether religiously based or not, have been ever present in song and literature alike.

Édouard Glissant, a poet and literary critic from the Caribbean island of Martinique, describes these inner histories as "opaque."[19] By this term Glissant means that the cultural differences of the Black Caribbean should not be explained to the world in terms of eighteenth-century style scientific reasoning. Black humanity, he says, is diminished when it is reduced or rigidly categorized. He argues that this way of viewing is a form of taxonomy, a way of categorizing humanity as a species branch. Opacity upsets "the hierarchy of this scale."[20] Black humanness no longer has to fit into a preconceived category of humanity defined by the West, which incidentally itself is not a monolith, but an imaginative fiction of militarized, industrial power. "The opaque," Glissant voices, "is not the obscure, though it is possible for to be so and accepted as such. It is that which cannot be reduced, which is the most perennial guarantee of participation and confluence."[21] In Glissant's estimation it is not necessary to devour other people in the idea that there is one kind of rational truth or universality. He writes,

I thus am able to conceive of the opacity of the other for me, without reproach for my opacity for him. To feel in solidarity with him or to like what he does, it is not necessary for me to grasp him. It is not necessary to try to become the other (to become other) nor to "make" him in my image.[22]

There is an important political dimension to this argument. Opacity provides legitimacy to both past and present group experiences. That is, their experiences must be considered on their own terms. Key in understanding this term is Glissant's conceptualization that there are plural experiences. These experiences cannot be papered over by one dominating ideology or sets of beliefs. The types of immigrant experiences into the Americas were not all the same. The saltwater experiences by the millions of transatlantic slaves were not same as those leaving Europe for better farmlands in North America. Glissant reflects:

> Only by understanding that is impossible to reduce anyone, no matter who, to a truth he would not have generated on his own. That is, with the opacity of his time and place. Plato's city is for Plato. Hegel's vision is for Hegel, the griot's town is for the griot. Nothing prohibits our seeing them in confluence, without confusing them in some magna or reducing them to each other. This same opacity is also the force that drives every community: the thing that would bring us together forever and make us permanently distinctive. Widespread consent to specific opacities is the most straightforward equivalent of nonbarbarism.[23]

Glissant's thoughts on opacity inform this book. Black American communities are as diverse internally as the individuals that comprise them. But there is also an important religious dimension to be considered. Part of this diversity has been expressed in individual understandings and how religion, as a set of formative experiences, ideas, hopes, and dreams, has been made operational. Religiosities in general, and Black religiosities specifically, have been opaque to American society writ large. Historically and sociologically, Black religiosity has been categorized or mischaracterized so as to make it virtually unrecognizable. Black religiosity has been depicted as racially romanticized in the form of the primitive or reduced to derogatory buzzwords such as childish, a psychologically disabling "opiate" and "fundamentalist."[24] Despite the reductionist renderings by those looking from the outside or those trying to give some account from the inside as to why some Black Americans hold a faith, the fact is that many persons within Black communities hold as well as exchange faiths. These faiths are the basis by which they use to tell or devise their stories. The stories are opaque, inner histories of a community being shaped and reshaped by an ever-changing world. As such, they are important to discern, discuss, and come to terms with.

This book explores the stories of four African American figures and their religious journeys through their autobiographical writings, interviews, speeches, letters, and memorable public performances. Ethel Waters, Mary Lou Williams, Eldridge Cleaver, and Muhammad Ali all shared their faiths publicly. For them, liberation was not simply defined by material or legal well-being, but by a spiritual search for community and personal wholeness. In a 1964 interview of Muhammad Ali, *New York Times* sportswriter Robert Lipsyte asked him about his decision to join the Nation of Islam (NOI). Ali remarked that the NOI was deeply moral. "I know where I'm going and I know the truth and I don't have to be what you want me to be. *I'm free to be what I want to be.*"[25] That sentiment, that brash assertion of self, informs and empowers each of the personalities profiled in this book. That personal assertion is as much of part of the twentieth-century story of Black America as was its mobilization against Jim and Jane Crow. (emphasis mine)

Ali's exchange with Lipsyte replicates why Glissant's notion of opacity is important. He declared his right not to have his religious persuasion reduced to a model of what was viewed as an "acceptable" religion by the dominant society. This would be equally true for the others described in these pages. Their religion or use of religion was both a moral behavioral code and a transcendent yielding of their persons to a greater life force. What they sought religiously was not reducible to repeated categorizations about the propriety of some faiths versus others.

Each of these figures used faith to reconcile deep personal struggles, voice their concerns for human dignity, and reinvent their public image. As a result, Waters, a nationally renowned blues and jazz singer, a famous stage and film actress (and a closeted lesbian/bisexual), was able to reinvent herself into an internationally recognized evangelical performer with the Billy Graham Crusade. Similarly, Williams's conversion to Catholicism aided her in overcoming an addiction to gambling and enabled her to later use her musical talents to find personal peace, while also challenging Rome and the American Catholic Church to recognize its complicit political and social involvement in slavery and racial segregation. Cleaver, a convicted rapist, became a spiritual seeker during his imprisonment, then a member of the NOI, which led him to emerge as a political radical and best-selling author. After being politically exiled from the United States, Cleaver converted publicly to American evangelicalism and then, in the later years of his life, converted once again to the Church of Jesus Christ of Latter Day Saints (Mormonism) while simultaneously joining the Republican Party. And, as noted, Ali's form of Islam gave him the courage to challenge his military draft status and become an international Black spokesperson as he inspired people all over the world.

These inner histories are faith stories, though inner histories are not always theistic. Their narratives belie a complicated relationship with the transcendent as the sociologist Nancy Ammerman spells out in her examination of everyday religion.

> Like all stories, narratives of everyday religion are complicated. They are multilayered, with character and plots interwoven across and with situations. Stories from one social arena are often transposed into another, so religious narratives may appear in settings outside officially religious bounds (and vice versa). More importantly, the stories we are looking for are neither purely spiritual and sacred and otherworldly, nor simply this-worldly and mundane.[26]

These stories of "everyday religion" read across faiths, generations, gender, and occupations to offer insights into the individuals' lives, and hopefully will lead to greater dialogues in the context of their broader communities' political histories. They explicitly avoid the disturbing tendency to flatten out in stereotypical parodies the lives of Black Americans. It is a history that is fashioned to make one stop, give pause, and to think about the meaning of their stories given their historical era. This inner history asks: How did their theism or antitheism structure their personal demons and best virtues? What did their search for sacred or social values say about their politics or the politics of their day? How did they reconcile their desires—what is pleasurable, psychically and sexually—in light of their faith and/or socially reinforced notions concerning taboo matters of pleasure? My argument here is that thinking and writing about the inner lives of these four figures, what I call the inner history, not only provides insights about these four individuals, but also gets us closer to understanding the pluralism that makes up the fabric of Black Lives. Through this examination it is my hope that we can get closer to appreciating our differences and creating democratic spaces where we can all find a comfortable place to inhabit.

This book owes a debt to religious scholar Charles Marsh's book *God's Long Summer: Stories of Faith and Civil Rights*. In 1997, Marsh did something amazing: he examined the faiths and the faith conflicts during the summer of 1964, known as "Freedom Summer." He interrogated the variety of ways that civil rights activists and anti-activists used faith in the South at one particular moment and time. His scholarship became a model for this book.[27]

I diverge from Marsh in that these inner histories reflect a pluralism even within Black Christian communities. Secondarily, my own story is so intertwined with these subjects that it would be disingenuous of me to pretend that this project is fully an objective history by a detached scholar.[28] I had encountered these individuals growing up through books, media, and performances so personally that I insert my own personal story into these narratives. I simply could not be a "distant narrator."

My consideration of an inner history is in part rooted in my own social location as a person. I grew up in a religious world—a world where religion was believed, lived, and intellectually engaged. Sacred and profane points of view were the stuff of constant conversations in my home, on the streets, at church, in the barbershop, and on public transportation. I spent my childhood in New

Orleans, immersed in that world. If Mardi Gras was a seven-day Bacchanalian festival in the Western liturgical calendar, then Lent was an introspective time, and the fecund Pagan Bunny became Christian each Easter Sunday where folk showed up, well dressed, at least once a year. And where would life be, in my New Orleans household, without discussions of working roots, Hoodoo, Voodoo, spells, and a child born with a caul or veil over its face? Religion and religious discussions were as much a part of my diet as were red beans and rice.

When I was fourteen, my mother and I left New Orleans and moved to Chicago. Chicago was an entirely different kind of religious world in an industrial city, then on decline, in 1970. Living in a predominately Black, middle-class enclave on the city's far southside, I discovered for the first time that the range of Black religiosity was even more expansive than what I had known in New Orleans. In our neighborhood, there were the faithful Muslim members of the NOI, Sunni, or Orthodox; the American Muslim Mission; Buddhists, Bahá'í faithful, and Yoruba cosmologists. The largest groups were Roman Catholics and Protestants and of those, Black Protestants made up the majority. Though there were all types of believers and faithful adherents, there was an outspoken minority within the communities in which I lived who were agnostic and openly atheistic. They rounded out the discussion about faith and belief, reminding believers that faith might be more fully rewarded by believing only in the here and now.

On a daily basis, the merits of religion followed my life up and down the Mississippi River from New Orleans to Chicago. It was a truism, and perhaps it still is, that spirituality and organized religion helped define what it meant to be an American, and most notably what it meant to live as a Black in America. Sociologically and historically there is enough evidence that one of the enduring organizational bases of politics among Black Americans are Protestant churches derived in part from the English Reformation, particularly those that are Baptist and Methodist. Any cursory read of nineteenth- and twentieth-century sources will note the great preponderance of evidence to support this empirically. The organizational units that Black Americans formed using a theologically informed discourse to partially unify its community and play moral jujitsu within a nineteenth-century slaveholding society and the industrializing global power of White supremacy is an amazing history in itself. Out of these organized traditions evolved other movements. Black Holiness and Pentecostal movements have had a worldwide influence in the twentieth and twenty-first centuries, and still remain undervalued. While Black church membership may not have as much influence as it once did, it continues to play a powerful role in the expression of Black humanity and its grievances against the governing forces of the United States that have labeled Blackness, or being Black, as sign of inhumanity. This is true collectively, but truer individually, where personal longing, desire, pleasure, dread, and despair, as well as madness and manias, are all complexly bundled existentially with a human time clock ticking down—we have just so many years.

So, it is out of my own social location that I attempt to examine the inner history surrounding these four persons. Their faith storying, like my own, is important to consider when we think about how we contemplate our world. Religion and faith do not seem to be going away anytime soon. Faith and faiths, religious as well as humanism, are used to inspire imperialisms, fashion warfare, provide cover for greed and abuses and, yet, at the same time faith and faiths are building blocks to democratic movements, provide forms of self-care, and build communities of people from cradle to grave.

Poet and writer Elizabeth Alexander in her collection of essays titled *The Black Interior* reminds the historian that we must imaginatively rethink about the sources that describe the realities of Black lives. She critically accesses that

African American people are seen, imagined, and "known" through sociological and fantasy discourses, but the troves of our culture offer enlightening angles of vision. The historian laments caesuras in the historical record; the artist can offer deeply informed imagining that, while not empirically verifiable, offers one of the only routes we may have to imagine a past whose records have not been kept precious. The artist may, in fact, jog the historian to think in new ways about the data he or she might gather.

Alexander goes further in her description:

The black interior, that is, black life and creativity behind the face of stereotype and limited imagination. The black interior is a metaphysical space beyond the black public everyday toward power and wild imagination that black people ourselves know we possess but need to be reminded of. It is a space that black people ourselves have policed at various historical moments. Tapping into this black imaginary helps us to envision what are not meant to envision: complex black selves, real and enactable black power, rampant and unfetishized black beauty. What do we learn when we pause at sites of contradiction, where black creativity complicates and resists what blackness is "supposed" to be? What in our culture speaks, sustains, and survives, post-nationalism, post-racial romance, into the unwritten black future we must imagine?[29] (emphasis original)

Alexander sees the black interior as a dream space, or, as she phrases it, "the great hopeful space of African American creativity." Her view is that "the black interior" is an "inner space in which black artists have found selves that go far, far beyond the limited expectations and definition of what black is, isn't should be."[30] Her idea shares W. E. B. DuBois's notion that Black people are workers in what he called in *Souls of Black Folk* the "kingdom of culture." These imaginings are faith acts. Having faith is an act of imagining. Black American encounters with religion was in fact a highly democratic, widely diffuse, expressive, and debatable set of imaginings. Religious ideas, rituals, spaces, and faiths always have been squares in the quilting of both subjectivity and community.

Religious scholar and humanist Anthony Pinn opines that religion is more than Christianity. He expands the notion of Black religion observing:

Simply put, religion is that which provides orientation or direction for human life, "for life in the world, together with motivation for living and acting in accordance with this orientation—that is, would gain, and gradually formulate, a sense of the *meaning* of human existence." . . . Therefore, religion at its core is a process of meaning-making. . . . Because of this framework, both *theistic* and *nontheistic* forms of religious expression and experience are religion because religion, simply understood, spreads beyond traditional boundaries of Christian formations. In short, religion entails "underlying resources of meaning and ritual that inform and fund the ongoing living and dying in a culture as a whole."[31] (emphasis original)

Yet, Black religious pluralism must be placed into historical perspective. Black American religious pluralism derived from the thick culture of Black Protestantism. Black Americans were a part of what historian Martin Marty described as the *Righteous Empire*.[32] Marty showed how Anglo-European Protestants used their faith doctrines as an ideological support for expansion and conquest in shaping the United States. By the 1830s, though socially antinomian, the descendants of captured Africans and enslaved Americans who were ostensibly Protestant also created religious, cultural, and political institutions. These fragile and oppressed institutions were "invisible" or hidden in some regions and marginalized in others. They, however, were as much a part of the wider nineteenth-century revivalist culture. Black Americans attended camp meetings and revivals for entertaining spirituality just as their White neighbors. Though Black Americans vitally shaped American Protestantism it cannot be forgotten that as Protestants they were the country's exploitable step children. The "Righteous Empire" was buttressed after all by the all-pervasive "peculiar institution," enslaved labor.

When slavery in the United States was abolished, Black Americans built upon their own Protestant foundations and initiatives. They did not have access to theological education or full control of their own institutions as they tried to break away from White Protestant dominance. They therefore shared with

White evangelicals a sacrosanct theological individualism. Meaning God's care for the person is tantamount through one's individual relationship to Jesus as Lord and Savior. This relationship to the Christ as revealed in the Bible was the measure of how regard for others was given and personal behavior deemed responsible. These notions were both systematized and inchoate. Arguably their worshipping settings provided its members and nonmembers with a cultural opacity too. They freed countless persons to live noble lives, but trapped countless others. For sociologist and social gospelers alike, these "otherworldly" tenets did not always cohere with political mobilizing to usher in the kingdom of God or bring a more just democracy to the body politics, or, so they believed.

Black Americans imaginatively used this evangelical logic to create institutions of their own making. They built under duress diverse institutions to exercise their own theological ideations. These were asymmetrical impoverished organizations. And until recently, they remained opaque institutionally and intellectually to a larger non-Black public. Organically they fostered indigenous leadership, created styles of cultural performance, and quilted together community building pieties and rituals. Though these institutions were noble in intent they could also be stifling. Too often individuals felt entrapped by their various conformities. This has always been the yin and the yang of institutions born in the eras of heightened racial violence and fears. In fact, all four persons in this book wrestle with the limitations of Black Protestantism. Empirically the majority of Black Americans continue to be Black Protestants. Black Protestantism has continuously undergirded American culture and is today a global influencer in Africa and Latin America. We cannot easily escape its foundational role whether we agree with its influences or not.

What became apparent to me when thinking about the four persons who are the subject of this book is how they all wrestled with their religious inheritances stemming from their Black Protestant worlds. They did this publicly by writing. These celebrity faith stories are a part of Black America's diverse communal archive. These writings are understudied by scholars as compared to the books penned by "secular" Black or religious intellectuals.[33]

The faith stories told between these pages aim to inspire both believers and nonbelievers to critically think about the opaque meanings of faith in daily existence. This book is not a pessimistic excavation. I do not view faith or faiths as solely compensatory or an opiate. Rather, my own hopeful inclinations in the vein of Howard Thurman are driven by a realization that in order to endure and engage in justice struggles one must possess and be aware of one's own faith. Perhaps, if we are aware that we have faith story too, we as Americans can learn how to build a stronger scaffolding for a more robust inclusive democracy. Rarely do writers, especially historians, say they explicitly wish to inspire anymore, fearing the ugliest forms of nativism. It is an understandable reticence. Yet, I would not be truthful if I did not say that this book seeks to inspire public conversations, debates, and discourses about democratic faiths. This really matters, especially in the United States, a country premised on its citizens being ideologically naïve about their own civil faiths. James Baldwin literarily condemned this kind of willful "innocence." For him Americans unexamined faiths daily meted out death sentences to Black America and by extension others around the world.[34]

So, consider this book an effort to recover a usable democratic past from the faith stories of four Black Americans. Maybe, just maybe, by examining these stories we might creatively recover moral possibilities for today. Amid authoritarian and antidemocratic politics, Islamophobia, ISIL, and justice struggles like Black Lives Matters, it seems a crucial time to examine faith stories. Historians, religious studies scholars, and social theorists place too much emphasis on demonstrating historical contradictions, whether personal or structural, in the hopes that it might lessen Americans' maleficent historical blamelessness. It never has. Perhaps, then, it is high time we took another tact.

Maybe our efforts should focus on how people in communities aspirationally "story" to expand their life options. Examining faith stories is one way of accomplishing this end. And this is significant, especially given that we increasingly live in a society that enslaves people around the globe through the technological inputs of an enchaining algorithmic calculus. And contemporarily this reality raises important questions regarding humanity. How do we picture ourselves? How do we escape social entrapments of capitalist technology in the framing of the self and self-worth? How do we imagine our worlds anew? Just, how do we resist *Stepford Wives* homogenization? In this book, the individuals told their stories through faith and faiths to address their struggles. Like my subjects, I, too, have grappled with issues of faith intellectually and as a daily discipline for living. This is why I have chosen to enter into a dialogue with them.

This is a different gambit on my part as a professional historian where objective distance is the rule of the discipline. Moving outside the confines of disciplinary protocols is, perhaps, well worth it given the age in which we live.

# 1

# I sing because I am free: Ethel Waters

The first time I saw Ethel Waters was on television as a ten-year-old. I knew nothing of her life's journey or her years of performing as an entertainment superstar. In that moment, I was simply a sullen kid being forced to watch a Billy Graham Crusade on television. It was excruciating since I wanted to watch either one of my favorite television series or a baseball game. Here was this joyous gray-haired matron smiling and singing before what seemed to be an ocean of White people. The lens through which I eyed her performance had been shaped by another performance on my streets and on the television, that of civil rights movement and the militancy of the Black Power demands.

I sternly judged Waters with all the sexist, self-righteous indignation that a thinking ten-year-old boy could muster. I resented her, as well as my maternal grandmother who forced me to endure Billy Graham, the evangelical revivalist on whose behalf Waters performed. In my eyes she was Aunt Jemima, the ubiquitously commercialized and fictional Black woman used to advertise syrup that I delightfully poured over my grandmother's homemade pancakes.[1] Looking back on this encounter with Ethel Waters, I am not sure who I truly resented more, her or my grandmother. In retrospect, I was torn because my grandmother came of age in the 1920s to Waters's music, dancing in an artful interpretation of the Blues and doing the shimmy, a predecessor to twerking. However, I would not learn about this aspect of my grandmother's life until much later. My grandmother, the person I knew, was a domestic in the home of a wealthy New Orleans physician and shared with Waters a strategy common in her generation of dissemblance, creating alternative narratives of self-recreation, in the face of what I now realize were lives bounded by sexualized racism and predatory sexual exploitation.

My grandmother thought watching Billy Graham (as well as at times Catholic Bishop Fulton Sheen) would add to my moral upbringing. Yet, the only thing I took away from that memorable encounter in my tween years was one that only the fictional cartoon character Huey Freeman from *The Boondocks* might have appreciated. For me, then, Ethel Waters's wide gap-toothed smile and her lifelong theme song "His Eye Is on the Sparrow" seemed in retrospect an inchoate misrepresentation of Black struggle and dignity. She might as well have been singing minstrel "coon songs" as far as I was concerned. However, no Black woman is as simplistic as my sexist memory.

Ironically, in 1999, the *New York Times Magazine* published a witty thought-provoking column titled "Irritating Women." Various women authors and cultural critics shared insightful paragraphs on historical women. Margo Jefferson, one of the *Times* cultural critics, brought Waters thunderously back to my mind in her paragraph. Jefferson's paragraph titled "Chameleon" gave me whiplash.

The most deliciously irritating thing about Ethel Waters—singer, dancer, actress, evangelist—was that she could never be confined to one identity. As a singer, she played with styles, doing what you might call vocal blackface and vocal whiteface. People still like to think that black and white styles can be firmly categorized; for Waters, they were only parts of a persona. She was born illegitimate in Chester, PA, on Halloween in 1896. She was a street kid whose highest aspiration was to be a lady's maid. Instead, she found herself in vaudeville. As an actress, in films like *The Member of the Wedding*, Waters gave so-called mammy roles real edge and depth. To some, her life was as irritating as her singing. She was a Catholic who could swear like a stevedore. She was a lesbian whose loud fights with her lovers made more proper lesbians like Alberta Hunter label her a disgrace to the tribe. In the early 70's she joined Billy Graham and toured the country. Her signature song had been "Stormy Weather," but once she joined Graham, she never sang it again. My life ain't stormy no more, she told people, which was good for her and bad for us.[2]

I was shocked! I supposed I should not have been. I thought I was fully cognizant of the complexities of Black women lives from my readings of Zora Neale Hurston, Ann Petry, Gayle Jones, Toni Morrison, Alice Walker, and other novelists whose writings reflected upon the innermost lives of their Black female characters. My PhD mentor and historian Darlene Clark Hine had also written about the struggles of Black women, but somehow, I never associated this struggle with Waters. In 1989, Hine wrote movingly of the personal disjuncture that Black women faced migrating from the South to the Midwest. She observed:

> Because of the interplay of racial animosity, class tensions, gender role differentiation, and regional economic variations, Black women, as a rule, developed and adhered to a cult of secrecy, a culture of dissemblance, to protect the sanctity of inner aspects of their lives. The dynamics of dissemblance involved creating the appearance of disclosure, or openness about themselves and their feelings, while actually remaining an enigma. Only with secrecy, thus achieving a self-imposed invisibility, could ordinary Black women accrue the psychic space and harness the resources needed to hold their own in the often one-sided and mismatched resistance struggle.[3]

Hine's insight in tandem with Jefferson's description of Waters forced me to rethink how I had youthfully considered my grandmother and Waters alike. She was not Aunt Jemima, but who was she? How did she survive as a Black woman, even an elite performer, in an era marked by everyday indignities reminding all Black persons of the constancy of their subordination? Given the struggles of her generation how did she account for her all-star success and longevity in a grinding entertainment industry that saw so many immense talented performers discarded as obscure historical footnotes? I wondered how she reconciled love, loves, and lovers in an American evangelical world where sex, not injustice, was and is the deadliest of sin? The Ethel Waters that I childishly made a snap judgment about after seeing her visual persona in the 1960s was far more complex than I could ever imagine.

More importantly, Jefferson's short assessment placed Ethel Waters's faith squarely in front of me. It led me to read Waters's memoir written with Charles Samuels titled *His Eye Is on the Sparrow*, and I was struck by the depth of her religious sentiment. I noticed, however, that her religious understanding was not confined simply to her encounter with Billy Graham, as Jefferson suggested. How might I think and engage her faith and religious understandings from her perspective? Why did she choose faith or did faith choose her in her "storying" of her struggles? Why did she choose to reveal so much of her inner turmoil in her best-selling memoir, published in 1950? Waters's public revelations about aspects of her personal life seem to have violated the historical use of dissemblance as a protective feature found in the lives of Black women of her generation.[4] Or did faith provide her a protective cloak that shielded, or perhaps strengthened, her inner self as she wrestled with the trauma of being a child born of a rape? Did faith help make her life more palatable as she struggled with a familial life conditioned by the stresses and resentments of impoverishment, stresses that burdened her all of her life? And just what was the content of her faith? It was never orthodox, meaning Waters never tried to fit her faith into a clerical discipline or doctrinal teachings. She was baptized Roman Catholic, loved what she called "old-time" Protestant religion with fiery oratory, robust Black hymnody, and camp meeting revivalist worship that began its development on the American slave frontier. She also supported a Catholic convent throughout her illustrious career in show business. And finally, what are we to make of her faith since she did not attend a regular worshipping congregation in Philadelphia, New York, or Los Angeles over the course of her adult life? To borrow from the scholar Marla Frederick, what was Waters's faith between Sundays?[5] Simply, how did she negotiate her faith as a sense of wonderment through worship and praise in her daily life? Frederick observes in a study of a group Black women located in North Carolina that spirituality, conceived as prayers and religious interactions, "is not only about the political negotiated within the public sphere. It is also about the everyday negotiated within the private sphere."[6]

Frederick's insight directed me to think about what Waters's piety and prayers meant to her as she attempted to cope with daily stresses. What were the issues that she struggled with privately? How did she cope with the frenetic life of being an entertainer? Did it aid her in the constant road travel, performing exhaustively night after night? How did she manage the expectation of her fans? Every night she was expected to be at her best as a singer and later a stage actor; how did she handle their disappointments? How did she cope with her open and closeted loves as well as the constant chatter of gossip concerning her celebrity? Further, how did she survive the fluctuations in her weight and the media commentary about her body? Was prayer a private way to keep her fierce temper and deepest insecurities at bay? And finally, did she feel the need to pray for her family members?

As her family's economic caretaker, Waters's life was topsy-turvy and constantly worrisome. She had been a working, poor Black girl-turned-woman and felt the injuries of class inflicted by the pretentiousness and self-importance of the middle class. Waters always resented "the dictys," as she called the Black middle classes, who shrouded themselves in with a veneer of public respectability, but secretly lived troubled lives. She resented those who looked their nose down upon people who grew up as she did on the streets and working less than respectable jobs to sustain themselves. Waters spent her fair share of time praying to forgive herself for her attitudes, but a fierce rage clung to her. The years of impoverishment constantly shadowed her. She never let go of the fighting and cussing she had to do to make her way through streets of Chester and Philadelphia and ultimately become a showstopping entertainer.

She had faith, but it was always interwoven with her memories of economic insecurity and class resentments.

Though economics was an overwhelming concern in Waters's life, her sexual preference for women was even more challenging in an era defined by normative notions regarding acts of sexual intimacy. How could a Black woman who was already an object of social derision in American society publicly express her pleasure and love for women as life-partners and sexual affection? The era of Waters's popularity was still dominated by a Victorian-era, religion-based sensibility about the proper role of sexuality. Protestant preachers and Roman Catholic priests were deeply concerned that the mass production of popular entertainment would lead to even more lascivious public immorality. And it was the queer world in particular where openness about sexual practices and unorthodox loves had to be suppressed. An evangelical conversion, or a Christian recommitment, or a Catholic confession were all defined in the minds of many clerics as turning the faithful away from hedonism through repentance. Theater history scholar James Wilson observed that a Harlem Seventh Day Adventist pastor, Elder M. C. Strachan, called playhouses the "Vestibules of Hell." Strachan preached:

> The popular playhouse of today has become the nursery of vice and the seminary of crime. As an institution, it is training the rising generation to be experts in degeneracy. The chief and most popular themes presented are wild and frenzied love, base and meaner passions, male lust and female shame, thrilling madness and murder.[7]

Waters had heard all the various sermonic jeremiads railing against the sins of popular entertainment. The irony of these condemnations was that they, too, worked well as great theatric entertainment.[8] These sermonic condemnations were equally staged for dramatic effect to wide audiences.[9] The symbiotic relationship between church and theater was never lost on her either. Yet publicly very few people spoke openly of same-sex love, though they lived it.

Discussions of queer love were only whispered or shared as open secrets in select clubs, a few churches, and among certain groups who kept it knowingly on the "down low."[10]

Recollecting Waters solely through the lens of her relationship to Billy Graham's Crusades, as Jefferson did in her short portrait, misses the fact that her lived faith did not bind her to a caricatured notion of evangelical conversion. Therefore, it begs the question, just what was her relationship to the American evangelical movement that began its ascent as her career was descending? What was her relationship to Graham, one of the United States' chief revivalist preachers and moralists in the late twentieth century? How did Waters and the Graham Crusade benefit from one another's religious performances? How did these two highly skilled stagehands deliberately stage racial integration, even as the national civil rights struggles and the 1968 *Kerner Report* exposed that the nation was "moving toward two societies, one black, one white—separate and unequal"?

Professionally Waters was deeply engaged and supportive of the struggles of Black Americans. She knew from her years of being treated as a second-class citizen the daily humiliation Black people experienced; being a prominent entertainer in her era did not shield her. She did a great deal of voluntary engagements to support civil rights causes, even when a segment of the civil rights leadership unduly criticized her and other Black entertainers for trying to make a living in a highly gendered and racist entertainment business. Though she was supportive, she seemed to be weary of the demonstration and demonstrative behaviors of assertive young Black people. In her senior years, she echoed Graham's anticommunist sentiments and disparaged youthful Black radicalism. For me this raised another question. I wondered how she reconciled herself to work with Graham's politics of White decency with Martin Luther King, Jr.'s nonviolent revolutionary theology.[11] The irony of Waters is that she made her first appearance with Graham at the only time that Graham and King appeared on stage together in 1957 at Madison Square Garden.

Jeffeson's pithy analysis forced me to rethink my boyhood judgments. As I thought about Waters's life forced me to recount my own autobiography, which included my adolescent participation in Black offshoots of Billy Graham–linked organizations around Chicago such as Youth for Christ, noted Black evangelical Tom Skinner's organization, William Bentley's National Association of Black Evangelicals, and my attendance for a year at an evangelical-related college, Trinity.[12] Like, Waters, I, too, shared a complex relationship with American evangelicalism throughout the 1970s. In point of fact, I had insider knowledge into the gestures, the theological codes of ethics and conduct that I grew weary of as I faced the challenges of religious pluralism and human suffering. Jefferson's paragraph alerted me that there was plenty I did not understand about Waters's journey of faith nor my own. So, I sought out her writings and what others wrote about her to try to understand her path as well as mine. I discovered that Waters had authored two memoirs: one a publishing sensation, the other not. The first one, *His Eye Is on the Sparrow*, published in 1950 was a compelling recollection of life on the stage and its demands and sacrifices; the other, *To Me It's Wonderful*, the evangelical one, published in 1972 was written less dramatically and from a more pious perspective that failed to reveal Waters's very human contradictions and complexity. However, the latter memoir offered insights to the wizened senior coping with the process of aging. Nevertheless, engaging both of these books alongside other accounts by her major biographer Donald Bogle helped me to fill in some of the blanks regarding her faith, her private self, and her public expressions of piety.

## "Ethel Waters and a Hymn"

When it was released in 1951, Ethel Waters's autobiography *His Eye Is on the Sparrow* was an immediate hit! It had been nationally picked up by the Book-of-the-Month Club and widely reviewed.[13] Her memoir, though religiously informed, was not written as a puritanical conversion narrative. In it, she does not identify *the* dramatic moment of conviction when her sins overwhelmed her and she accepted desolate unworthiness, absolving into God's love. For Waters, her storying of "turning" or repentance, as the Puritans termed it in the seventeenth century, was a bricolage, a moral mixtape of Black Protestantism and Catholicism.[14] For Waters, faith in God was a constant moral force that kept and guided her through successes and trials. From the beginning, God was with her.

Waters explained her rationale for writing her memoir in an interview with *New York Times* reporter Harvey Breit. She opined:

> It is no book. . . . It is my life. There is no mechanics. You don't live a life span and say it in one paragraph or in one line. There's nothing commercial or melodramatic in it. I told my life story to stop people from having curiosity, to stop them from having to ask me questions, from wanting them to know my life so that maybe if could help somebody.[15]

Breit never asked Waters why people were curious about her life. Did she mean that people were curious about her life because she was a celebrity? What aspects of her life did she want a reading public and her fellow entertainers to know? In her conversation with Breit she elaborated:

> It's not a Negro. . . . It's a human story. Things have happened to me that have happened to every people and race in the world. The only miraculous thing is that God's hand kept me above it. The credit is only to God's helping me. But don't misunderstand me. My life was not sorrowful—it was all right and still is. . . . Would I want to live my life over again? Yes, I'd say yes.[16]

Throughout the interview Waters used pieties to address her formative difficulties or her skills as a singer and actress. Breit asked her if fending "for herself as a youngster helped later on as an actress." Though Waters was an immensely talented actor on film and stage she responded:

I'm not an actress. . . . I'm never acting. Everything I am able to portray on the stage I've fitted it from my life. I've given out to the theatre what came out of my life. Whatever I have to do I've been. I'm reliving my experience. I was brought up a Catholic. I'm a Catholic, a Baptist, a Methodist, I'm everything that's to help people.[17]

Breit's interview with Waters was somewhat disjointed. However, her book written with the assistance of Charles Samuels provided vibrant testimony.

From the very outset of her autobiography, Waters had been reflective. In 1951, though she claimed a stage age of fifty-one she was actually fifty-seven. At that time, she was at the pinnacle of entertaining success in recordings, stage, film, and television—only the second African American woman to have been nominated for a Hollywood Oscar. Publishing her memoir was, for her, the icing on the cake. Waters's autobiography was a faith narrative that began with an assessment of her life as a woman coming to grips with economic destitution and racial confinement as a Black girl.

I was never a child. I was never coddled, or liked, or understood by my family. I never felt I belonged. I was always an outsider. I was born out of wedlock, but that had nothing to do with all this. To people like mine a thing like that just didn't mean much. Nobody brought me up. I just ran wild as a little girl.[18]

According to Waters, she was an unwanted child, which explained her "outsider" status within the family. Her birth was the result of her teenage mother's rape. The only person who truly cared for her was her grandmother, an overworked live-in domestic, who came home on weekends fatigued and exhausted. Waters's family was composed primarily of women: her mother, grandmother, and two aunts who were economically impoverished. Their household as a collection of women appeared to have deep struggles along numerous lines. They struggled with the men in their lives to be lovingly accepted as partners and/or wives. Her two aunts, Vi and Ching, from Waters's description appear to have unsuccessfully fought with the ravages of alcoholism, an alcoholism no doubt in part linked to grief at the death of two of her cousins. Her Aunt Ching had two children, Myrtle and Tom; the former died in infancy and cousin Tom died of meningitis. In addition, this household of women struggled with interfamily stigma. According to Waters her grandmother's siblings were "snobbish" toward Waters's household. Undoubtedly, grandmother Sally Anderson's family, like many Black families, fought valiantly against the harshness of poverty. Anderson's household of women was in a constant state of economic flux, just as other poor families, and there were only so many resources available to share. It should go without saying that as Black female domestic workers, Anderson and her daughters were the cheapest of all laborers.[19] Waters poignantly remembered her grandmother's laboring status:

> In her whole life Mom never earned more than five or six dollars a week. Being without a husband, it was hard for her to find any place at all for us to live, a place she could afford. And even then, she never got a chance to live with my aunts and me, could only visit us on her day off.

Her daughters resisted Anderson's type of domestic employment. They rejected this kind of work as Waters explained: "Vi and Ching and Charlie took no interest in that. Mom might as well have tried to read poetry to cows."[20] What Waters did not articulate was how difficult it was for Black women in her grandmother and aunts' era. Historian Jacqueline Jones reflecting on Black women's labor history writes,

> As paid labors became increasingly associated with the time-oriented production of goods, the black nurse, maid, and cook remained something of a labor-force anachronism in a national if not regional (southern) context. A traditional form of "women's work"—dirty, tedious, low-paying— service lacked the rewards of self-satisfaction and pride that supposedly accompanied such tasks when performed for one's own family.

Jones trenchantly observed that the system of paid household labor itself undermined the Black woman's own role as mother and homemaker. Moreover, service made manifest all the tensions and uncertainties inherent in the personal interaction between the female members of two different classes. Black women both north and south "eagerly sought factory jobs that paid more money for shorter working hours and they lacked the social stigma attached to domestic service." (Jones, 154)[21] Vi and Chang resisted this kind of labor.

The wages taken home were a pittance. Black women's poverty as result of their low wages was consequential to family life. Waters recollected that she "was shuttled about among relatives, boarded out, continually being moved around to Camden, Chester, and Philadelphia homes."[22] To Waters, faith in God was key to her girlhood survival.

> Whatever moral qualities I have, come, I'm afraid from all the sordidness and evil I observed firsthand as a child. However, I do not wish to exaggerate the impact on me of the evil that constantly surrounded me when I was little. I was tough always and, like all slum kids, was able quickly to adjust myself to any and all situations. God's hand must have closed over me very early in life, making me tough and headstrong and resilient. It is His hand that carried me safely down the long, dark road I've had to follow since.[23]

Waters's institutional religious affiliations as a Roman Catholic began as a young child. Having contracted typhoid, she nearly died. As she explained her grandmother was inclined to Catholicism, though her daughter and Ethel's mother Louise Anderson never was baptized.[24] Perhaps Anderson viewed Catholicism as being more respectable than the many versions of Black Protestantism. Anderson's work required her to stay in the homes of employers and perhaps their middle class religiosity rubbed off. Waters believed that her grandmother spent so much time with White people that "she stopped living colored, thinking colored."[25] It was grandmother, whom she called Mom, who "sent for Father Healey of St. Peter Claver R.C. Church. He baptized and anointed me."[26] St. Peter Claver in Philadelphia began officially serving Black citizens around 1888 after the Archdiocese purchased the formerly Fourth Presbyterian Church at Twelfth and Lombard Streets.[27] The building was dedicated in 1892. The parish would serve a variety of Philadelphia's Black families over the course of its nearly 100-year history. The church was named after Peter Claver (1581–1654), a Spanish Jesuit priest, who for thirty-five years consoled African slaves in their lifetime fate as they arrived in Cartagena, Columbia.[28] Claver, who considered himself a "slave of slaves," was beatified by Pope Pius IX in 1850, and was canonized by Leo XIII in 1888. In the summer of 1896, after *Plessy v. Ferguson* was ruled upon in the United States Supreme Court, and the same year of Waters's birth, Claver was proclaimed the special patron of all the Catholic missions among Negroes with a feast day celebrated on September 9.[29] Anderson might not have known about the man Peter Claver, but St. Peter Claver Roman Catholic Church appeared to her to be more spiritually enlightening than various forms of Black Protestantism, which emphasize believers' baptism by consent and freedom of conscience. In Anderson's mind, St. Peter Claver was of a higher social status than Philadelphia's Black-led Protestant churches associated with the Black poor.

Waters grew up in an era of fierce denominational loyalties.[30] At stake was a historical debate about the theological merits of Protestantism and Catholicism, and which was more normative to American democracy. The ritualized routines of mass, the repetition of prayers, and the recitations of creeds in Catholicism seemed to many Protestants not a lived experience of God, as the Roman Catholic Church through the priest served as intermediary between the believer and God. In the Protestant orb no person stood in the way of God or Jesus Christ. There was a more direct connection via Bible reading, prayer, and congregational gatherings. The believer could experience God directly, as directly as one could experience a parent. This was all the more important for many Black Protestants where self-freedom was highly prized. It allowed one to move outside the gaze of slavery's oppression and apartheid's White dominance.

According to Waters, mother Louise never approved of her baptism as a Roman Catholic. There were tensions between Sally and Louise over Ethel's religious affiliation. As a result, the young Ethel seemed to be conflicted by her grandmother and mother's loyalties. However, as she explained, "The greatest thing in my whole childhood happened to me when I was nine. . . . The rock and the light I found was the Catholic Church." Waters began attending the school that was founded to serve the children of St. Peter Claver around 1905. As a troubled child, she found love and patience from her teacher Sister Mary Louise Agnes. Throughout her difficult childhood, attending St. Peter Claver's school was a bright spot. "I would leave the school full of hope and feeling exalted," she explained only to return home to her aunts who were consumed with alcohol, which kept them vexed and quarrelsome. "Louise," she told writer Samuel Williams, "never approved of my Catholicism and didn't let me stay in the school for very long."

> My mother never drank heavily. Old-fashioned religion was her refuge. I've always felt that I inherited her deeply religious feelings, but her conception of God was nothing like mine. Louise went in for the old backwoods, down-home religion, closely resembling that of the Holy Rollers and the Hard-Shall Shell Baptists. Louise painted God almost as an ogre. To her He was principally an avenging Spirit. Only a thin line was drawn between Him and the devil. I felt that God loved me as I loved Him. To me He was never a tyrant, an enemy just waiting to pounce if I made some mistake. Mom always challenged Louise's whooping and hollering religion. "You don't have to holler so," she'd say. "God has very big ears. He can hear you even if you whisper."[31]

Enervating as her personal struggles and impoverishment were, Waters's household nevertheless found solace in attending church, a familial routine.[32]

Church attendance did not ease the debate between her grandmother and mother over what kind of church she should affiliate with. They were torn between Protestantism and Catholicism. However, for Ethel, who always held onto to her Catholicism, she learned broader truths about herself at age eleven and the community in which she lived. Attending the Black Protestant communions that her mother approved of taught Waters that faith as expressed through denominational loyalties had something to teach. "What I learned going to" [Methodist and Baptist] "churches was that other religious than mine held something worthwhile and exalting."[33] In a world where Black people were exploited, silenced and play-acted being dumb, small Black congregations allowed them to be freely expressive, a freedom of the self.

> The beauty that came into the tired faces of the very old men and women excited me. All week long so many of them were confused and inarticulate. But on Sundays, in the church, they had no difficulty expressing themselves both in song and talk. The emotion that had invaded them was so much bigger than they. Some would rock. Some would cry. Some would talk with eloquence and fire, their confusion and doubts dispelled. And, oh, those hymns!

Waters developed her own sense of catholicity, her personal universality, through the tensions of Sally and Louise. She made a discovery about the commonness of life and the love that faith could bring to people. "It began to dawn on me," she observed, "that if sordidness left a deep and lasting mark, so could the goodness in life." Interacting in between ritual spaces of Black Protestant and Catholic she felt herself "getting close to God." In these settings, she never "could accept all the doctrine preached. My logic, my reasoning powers made me question much of the doctrine."[34] Young Waters found universal goodness and meaningfulness in all forms of Christian expression.

Waters's faith confirmation began as she described it in a revival meeting for children led by the Reverend R. J. Williams. Her self-description of this incident in her was in the salvific language that most American Protestant evangelicals would understand. She told Charles Samuels, "My search for God and my finding of Him were to begin in one of those Protestant churches where they were having a children's revival. It was there that I came to know and to reverence Christ, the Redeemer." She attended the revival "religiously," though she refused, unlike her friends, to take a seat on the "mourners' bench" upon Reverend Williams's appeal. Even when she went to pray with the Reverend she "didn't feel purged of sin or close to the Lord." Nevertheless, she continued to attend the revival. She recollected:

> On the last of the three extra nights of the meeting I got down on the mourners' bench, down on my knees once more. And I told myself, "If nothing happens tonight, I'll not come back again." Nobody had come that night to the meeting, nobody but the very old people who were always there. I was praying hard and hopefully, asking God, "What am I seeking here? What do I want of You? Help me! If nothing happens, I can't come back here anymore!" And then it happened! The peace of mind, the peace I had been seeking all my life. I knew that never again, so long as I live, could I experience that wonderful reaction I had that night in the little church. Love flooded my heart and I knew I had found God and that now and for always I would have an ally, a friend close by to strengthen me and cheer me on.[35]

Central to faith narratives are spiritual awakenings. Waters's awakening was bounded by the all too familiar recitations of sociological categories— economic deprivation, racism, and sexism. As she knew, her story was all too common; there was nothing exotic about being an impoverished girl child in the world. However, it was her spiritual sense of self that gave her commonplace life transcendence. As Marla Frederick points out, there are both public and private boundaries to Black women's spirituality.

> That women see their spirituality as central to their life experiences speaks to the power of spirituality to transform meaning and create action. Spirituality

is thus embedded in the "timeless" spaces. It is that which gives meaning to life's experiences, both its joys and sorrows. . . . The boundaries are not neat, nor are the categories that stable. There exist instead various manifestations of spirituality over the course of time. This is to say that both time and space impact how one interprets spirituality and how one chooses to live it out.[36]

The ever-shifting boundaries of spirituality kept Ethel Waters alive.

Waters's spiritual relationship to institutional churches was therefore based on utilitarian needs and self-care. She lived in a community where Black denominations held a highly respected place, but could not exercise exclusive control over their communities. In a racial economy where Blackness was stigmatized, Black Catholics could not escape or dominate Black Protestants just as Protestants could dismiss neither Holiness churches nor groups associated with the "near East" nor Islam.

Waters's Black world had an opulent catholicity. Though a self-declared Catholic, she found mystical resonance singing spirituals, evangelical Protestant hymnody, and gospel, not the least of which was a gospel song written by Charles H. Gabriel and Civilla D. Martin. That song, which she chose as the title of her autobiography, was *His Eye Is on the Sparrow*.

Singing Gabriel and Martin's song as a part of her repertoire became a powerful, if not nostalgic, ode to Ethel's grandmother's love. She understood its heart-tugging sentiments and power for her the singer, as well as her audiences that she so deeply moved by her renderings. As she recollected, it was her grandmother Sally's favorite. Waters learned to love it too, she wryly remembered, because her grandmother made her "stay in and play it for her one-finger on the organ, I wasn't singing because I was happy, I was singing because I had to."[37] Nevertheless this song came to represent her core self, the self away from inquiring minds of critics, theatrical rivalries and jealousies, and the constant touring. For Waters, singing "His Eye Is on the Sparrow" conjured up the divine making interior room for peace, forgiveness, compassion, and enduring strength.

## "I never been a promiscuous woman"

Ethel Waters portrayed her life as imperfectly heterosexual in her telling to Charles Samuels. She described her complex attraction to roughnecks, men whose earnings came from the underground economy and who were resistant to the snide politics of being respectable. "When it came to the men in her life," biographer Donald Bogle writes, "Ethel, she preferred the slick, highly sexed smooth-talkers with a street sophistication, who educated themselves through life experiences, not necessarily by reading books at college."[38]

Waters's relationship to men was always sticky. Worse, though, was her mother who consented to her being married at age thirteen to Merritt "Buddy" Purnsley, who was twenty-three. One can only wonder if Louise Anderson's trauma played into her consent; after all Anderson was thirteen when her daughter was born. Their brief marriage was harrowing. At thirteen she was unprepared emotionally or sexually. "Having seen so much of the ugly side of life as a little girl," she noted, "I dreaded the sex relationship. Yet I knew that sex had to happen to me as to everyone else. My wedding night could not have been nastier or more unpleasant." From its inception, the marriage was marred. That did not stop Waters from being a good "Catholic" by trying to be "a good wife." The moral teachings of Catholic Church on marriage thoroughly indoctrinated her with Marian-like principles about being a subservient female and wife. However, Buddy's brute patriarchy and physical abuse gave the lie to some of the church's teaching. His mistreatment of Waters was done to hide his relationship with another woman. Waters determinedly left Buddy after threatening his life. She told Charles Samuels, "At thirteen I was married, and at fourteen I was separated and on my own."[39] With her beloved grandmother deceased and a complex relationship with her mother, Waters began to dream of performing on stage as a way of escape.[40] The open and independent road of the entertainer attracted her as it did countless other young people. Vaudeville and the "Chitlin' Circuit" would be her bridge away from impoverishment.

In her memoir, Waters describes her intimate relationship with men as continuously challenging. She spoke of the danger of a young woman on being on the road with unscrupulous men attempting to drug and then gang rape her.[41] Yet she expressed her attraction to wizened street men like West Indian Johnny, a man twice her age,[42] and to Rocky her drug-addicted lover. Her love relationships with men were never conventional. Waters's tough life made her always suspicious of romantic heterosexual love. What attracted her to Rocky was the melodrama of their relationship. It was akin to a Spanish-speaking telenovela.

> Being a child of the underworld, the Jekyll-and-Hyde character of my boyfriend fascinated me more than it shocked me. When high, nobody could be more pleasant, and courtly and attentive than Rocky. But off the stuff, he was cross and irritable. But like most girls who are caught on the well-baited hook called love, I found it impossible to walk out. There was another reason why I stayed with him as long as I did. Watching him intrigued me, held the same excitement and suspense most people find in murder stories and blood-and-thunder melodramas. I couldn't wait to find what was going to happen next. And I was *living* my melodrama, not just losing myself in other people's make-believe. Rocky turned out to be a three-letter man as a junker. He took C, H, and M. In dopehead language C means cocaine, H heroin, and M morphine.[43] (emphasis original)

For a Christian of any stripe, whether Catholic or Protestant, Waters stepped outside the bounds of sexual conformity. She told Charles Samuels, "My attitude toward various men I've loved has always been the same. If my man told me he had other women, I didn't mind. But if he had other women and didn't tell me, I felt deceived and double-crossed and got into a fury." Her views defied the stereotypical Catholic Marian principle of the dutiful mother and virgin. For Waters, it was transparently clear that "it was never the act of infidelity that mattered so much as the cheating and lying part of it."[44] She gave her intimate male partners wide latitude, accommodating a form of nonconformist patriarchy, as long they were forthcoming about their other female partners with her in advance. Indeed, the range of her intimate habits was generationally a "Blues" one,[45] which Donald Bogle accents.

> In an environment where sex in the red-life districts was always available, where attitudes about sex were quite different from those of the ofays and the dictys, her sex education began at age of three, when she slept "in the same room, often the same bed, with my aunts and transient uncles. I was fully aware of what was going on." Though she professed to have no interest in sex, there was nothing about it that she didn't know by the age of seven. As a young woman, she also enjoyed going to the drag shows, where female impersonators were dressed in high fashion. Throughout her life, she would always view sex rather casually and without moral judgments. At an early age, no doubt, she was exposed to same-sex relationships as much as heterosexual ones, yet she never considered one type of sexual liaison more moral than another.[46]

Waters lived openly within the confines of Black entertainment, with an "don't ask, don't tell" attitude in regard to the sexual fluidity among individuals in the larger community.[47] Same-sex practices were openly known.[48] She lived a sexually liberated life in that sense. Many people like her, who left the South in her era and trekked North during the years of the Great Migration, sought anonymity to live quietly as free sexual persons. Big cities in the industrial North seemed to allow more space than more conservative Southern cities and towns steeped in Protestant literalism and judgmental scorn with the exception of, perhaps, New Orleans. Her own sexuality as a woman interested in same-sex love does not, however, appear in *His Eye Is on the Sparrow*. Her women intimates do not make the page in the same way as her male intimates. Nor did her youthful penchant for dressing in what was deemed male attire and fondness for Harlem's drag shows. In an era of political containment, when *His Eye Is on the Sparrow* was published, it disclosed information about her sexuality that was in the bounds of belief regarding the meaning of family.[49] She, after all, was a show business star and a certain bohemianism was expected. However, it was no secret among her entertainment peers and within her circle of intimates that Waters had women lovers who were closer to her than her male lovers. This begs the question: What does that say about Waters's faith?

Western Christendom had reinforced heterosexual relationships as being ethically normative for centuries and the church's doctrinal view of sexual normalcy influenced daily thinking about sexuality and human biological reproduction. This regularity began in the high Middle Ages and was heavily influenced by notions of natural law derived from the philosophy and theology of Thomas Aquinas. Protestants, too, did not abandon scholastic logic regarding nature during the Reformation either. This meant that sex as pleasure was frequently associated with male hedonism, which meant that Catholic Priests and Protestant clerics defined "natural" sex via male dominance. They replicated the social hierarchy and sex was enjoined solely for the reproduction of the species. Broadly speaking being queer was outside the bounds of nature. Scholastic thinkers, in a quest to control moral conduct, promoted sex as shameful and reinforced male asceticism in regard to sexual pleasure. Protestants, though affirming marriage more positively, would struggle to differentiate their views from their Catholic rivals in Europe. Though sexual relationships would be seen more favorably than in Catholicism, sexuality was squarely placed only inside the confines of marriage, that men dominated.[50] In contrast, the bodies of Africans and other colonial subjugated people were intentionally made exotic and eroticized in the extreme, defined as wild by nature, which was very useful in justifying transatlantic slavery.[51]

Waters's sexual openness defied the doctrinal patriarchy of Catholic and Protestant teachings. In her mind, God loved her no matter who her intimates were or were not. In herself she commanded a freedom that clerical teachings could neither dictate nor erase. Her relationships were not unnatural. As a human being she enjoyed sex with men, but in the main with women; how could God hate her for that? Waters's earliest positioning as a poor Black American girl surviving the bottom rung of a Chaucerian-like tale fueled her independence of mind and taught her lessons about power. She expressed her social resentments in terms of race and class not so much in terms of gender or being a woman, although she was cognizant that all three impinged upon her. Reflecting on poverty she observed:

> But then, all my life I've been prejudiced against wealthy people. No one has ever been able to convince me that Park Avenue folks are as good as my Tenth Avenue friends. . . . Poverty works like a steam roller, crushing a lot of people. But, like the steamroller, it's also a great leave. In the slums, you find out early in life that if you get hungry enough you'll do anything for a meal. Even after you had the breaks you remember that. Unless you're a complete phony, you never find it possible to think of yourself superior to those who haven't had your luck. You can't even despise thieves. You can only pity them because the jails are so big and strong and always crowded with poor, hungry, desperate men just like them.[52]

From lived experience Waters held a *Three Penney Opera*–like class analysis that the German composers Bertolt Brecht and Kurt Weill might have appreciated.

Waters's view of poverty was interconnected to how she had been raised. "I keep learning more about racial prejudice all the time," she told Williams. "My biggest surprise of all," she said, "has been the reaction of white people who wear their tolerance like a plume when I tell them I've never minded even slightly being a Negro." Twenty years before James Brown put the rhythmic high-hat drums onto the verses of *Say It Loud, I am Black and I'm Proud*, Waters expressed deep-rooted pride in Black people, which she derived independently in her theological reflections. "We are close to this earth and to God," she noted. "Shut up in ghettos, sneered at, beaten, enslaved, we have always have answered our oppressors with brave singing, dancing, and laughing." She continued, "Our greatest eloquence, the pith of the joy and sorrow in our unbreakable hearts, comes when we lift up our faces and talk to God, person to person. Ours is the truest dignity of man, the dignity of the undefeated." Waters was always class-conscious. She never forgot that she came from a Black female working-class. She reminded a *New York Post* reporter Earl Wilson at the height of her earning capacity that "she used to work from 9 to unconscious."[53]

It is forgotten today that Ethel Waters performed Irving Berlin's *Suppertime*, the powerful song about American lynching in the Broadway musical revue for *As Thousands Cheer*. The lyrics of the song poignantly tells the story of a woman who wishes to set the dinner table, but her husband who has been lynched will not be coming home for dinner.

How'll I keep explainin' when they ask me where he's gone?
How'll I keep from cryin' when I bring their supper on?
How can I remind them to pray at their humble board?
How can I be thankful when they start to thank the Lord?[54]

Waters embodied the song's lyrics and embraced it as a defiant telling of what she had seen in her own southern travels and a testimony to her people's suffering. *Suppertime*, as her chief biographer Donald Bogle observes, "marked an important shift in mainstream culture. Here in popular song, a social, racial, and political issue received comment."[55] So much would be made of the 1939 Billie Holiday's recording of the poem *Strange Fruit* written by Abel Meeropol, but Waters's performance six years before Holiday's song was equally compelling and a reality check in an era of escapist entertainment on Broadway and in Hollywood. She sang the song with an eye to ongoing lynchings occurring through the 1930s from Mississippi to Indiana. And she sang it with a particular eye and care toward nine young men charged of rape in the Alabama town of Scottsboro. She never attempted to escape being a

Black woman or demanding justice for her people. *Suppertime* was every bit as powerful as *Strange Fruit* and when she performed it on Broadway she stopped the show. As she explained, "If one song can tell the whole tragic history of a race, *Supper Time* was that song. In singing it. . . . I was telling my comfortable, well-fed, well-dressed listeners about my people."[56]

Waters did not hate White people; rather she viewed various kinds of White racists as people to be pitied and "in deep trouble." Her scorn, however, was reserved for the Dictys, the judgmental Black Middle Class!

> Dictys and the others among my own people who despise Negroes who are poor and ignorant and condemned to live like animals arouse my fury as no white people ever can. We Negroes have lived through so much together— centuries of slavery, terror, segregation, and unending concentrated abuse— that I'll never understand how some of us who have one way or another been able to lift ourselves a little to knock the hell out of our own blood brothers and sisters.[57]

Yet, lingering behind her class resentments and her distrust of White people was Waters's Catholic piety. In her ten-room suite at 115th and Morningside Ave in Harlem kept a Roman Catholic–style prayer room. *New York Post* reporter Earl Wilson observed the room this way:

> In it there is a small shrine where she frequently goes to kneel and the walls are religious images, religious medals and religious communications some framed. She has set aside this room of piety because some years ago she found herself burdened by a trouble which would not lift. She besought the Catholic sisters of a Carmelite nunnery near Allentown, PA, for spiritual counsel and was comforted. She began contributing to the institution; later she established this the religious room as her small place of worship. "I don't go to church like some people," she says. "I only go when there's nobody there but me and the church. I just go and sit and float away."[58]

If there was the cussing-and-fighting class resentful Waters, there was also the contemplative Ethel. Her "religious room" was her sacred space not bound by church rituals.[59] The Carmelites found its charge following the rich legacy of St. Teresa of Avila who was born into the world of the missionary zealotry of Conquistadores in the Americas and the tumultuous civil unrest inflamed by Luther's sixteenth-century Protestant revolution, loving Jesus and envisioning the Virgin as a way to harmonious equanimity. In Allentown, Pennsylvania, her disciples, monastery cofounders Mothers Mary Therese and Clement Mary, would come from Naples, Italy, to reside and follow in St. Teresa's mission. These Carmelite nuns were acquainted with the hardscrabble lives of working-class people, especially women.[60] When they arrived in the United States these sisters were open and amazingly moved beyond the straightjacket of racialized ethnicity to provide Waters with the care she needed. As result the monastery's mission would always be for Waters a cherished place, one that she remembered consistently donating to as a sign of her gratitude.

In Waters's retelling of her story she stayed within the bounds of the acceptable. She never veered away from the formal sexual propriety of her Cold War–era audiences, though she was open about race. Her memoir sold widely. Waters conformed to the dominant narrative in her published story, but in reality, she lived spiritually free in herself as a proud Black woman who loved women and men.[61] She was a working entertainer; her life and livelihood were on stage.

# It sounded so real

Ethel Waters's relationship to the Reverend Billy Graham was a staged one. Not that she did not fervently believe in God or the mission of the Graham Crusade—she did—but that she looked at Billy Graham and his crusade through a lens of performance. Since childhood Waters had assessed the performative side of religion, particularly Protestant preachers. In a bold observation Waters told Williams that early in life "I came to love and value the inner fire of a brimstone-and hellfire preacher. I sensed that there was something splendid about this kind of religion that exploded in the pastor's heart, enabling him to reach you and make you believe."[62] She understood the theatricality of Protestant preaching. She remembered that Reverend R. J. Williams who spiritually awakened her "had some compelling force in him that enabled him to contact people." She shrewdly compared his force to that of an actor. "Great actresses and statesmen and other popular idols have that same force, but great preachers most of all. He could soothe you and calm you and also stir you to the depths of your soul with what lay in his eyes, his voice, and his heart."[63] She saw the same charismatic theatricality in the young Billy Graham that she had seen in her adolescent memory of Reverend Williams.

Theatricality had always been part of American evangelicalism from the eighteenth century with the evolution of George Whitefield. Staging, self-promotion, and emotion-filled preaching lit the fields of the faithful afire, burning them over and becoming a mainstay of American Protestant culture.[64] Billy Graham was in a broader historical path that weaved itself down from Whitefield to Dwight Moody to Billy Sunday to Aimee McPherson and every unnamed revivalist who did not gain mass media attention, but who tried. If anything, Waters knew about Graham; he was above else a great showman. Reverend Graham and his team knew how to stage his message effectively and he used his charisma and dynamism to great effect in conveying his sermons. Like his English predecessor, Whitefield, Graham was a divine dramatist. One of Whitefield's biographers, Harry Stout, makes an important observation about the relationship of theater to the rise of American evangelicalism.

For centuries, the stage and the church had stood in mortal combat for the souls of their nation. Both encouraged a suspension of belief in the experience of the everyday to introduce their viewers to different worlds. Theater, its capacity to combine pageantry of art, the intensity of poetry, the enchantment of fiction, and the movement of dance, represented a religious-like amalgam of art and energy that as one contemporary put it, had the power "to get Possession of the heart."[65]

Whitefield became an actor-preacher and "passion" would be key to his sermonizing. Stout notes that implicit in his preaching were the same qualities that attracted Waters to impassioned preaching throughout her life. "Theater-driven preaching," Stout opines, "was an implicit model of human psychology and homiletics that saw humankind less as rational and intellectual than as emotive and impassioned."[66] It was the moved heart that was the test of true religion. For Waters, Graham could move hearts, which was her standard for judging preacher authenticity.

Waters's years on stage helped her to understand the kinesis of stardom, though Graham had been "puffed up," or in today's parlance "blown up" by William Randolph Hearst's newspapers by the 1950s. Hearst's publicity helped make Graham, ever the great showman, a national star. Waters had read the newspapers going in between Los Angeles and New York and heard him on the radio.

Waters knew a star when she saw it. In 1970, she gave testimony to her awareness of Graham's showmanship. She explained to Lois Fern in Baton Rouge, Louisiana, how she viewed the evangelist.

> No, when I first heard him there was something about him that sounded so good; it sounded so real. But I had been fooled before. And the next thing I had against him: he was white. I didn't think any white preacher could be that good. Now, I'm not a militant, never was one and can't stand them. Then he was young; I didn't know that then until I had seen him on TV a long time ago, coming out from Minneapolis. . . . He's not an intellectual preacher because God put it on the line for everybody to understand. . . . And there are so many people who study just big words and they don't know themselves what they are saying. There's nothing wrong with c-a-t is cat. That's why I always have loved him; when he says a thing you understand it.

That's his gift. And then there's something compelling: God speaks through him. You can tell his voice is compelling, and that wasn't acquired; that wasn't got in no seminary, God gave it to him, and no one can take it from him. He is one of God's children.[67]

In the interview Waters couched her comments in evangelical nomenclature. She emphasized that the key to Graham's renown was youth, clarity, and compelling voicing. He had the winning combination. Waters understood all this as a singer that the voicing had to appear authentic and compelling for an audience to grasp it. She also was aware that stardom was youth power. Popular icons garner power when they are young, as she did in her youth.

Central to the staging of the Waters-Graham relationship was race. The Bern interview unwittingly revealed this dimension. Ever attuned, Waters signals to her Black audience her distrust of Graham's whiteness, which she overcame with her belief that he had been sent by God as well as his singular personality. Throughout *His Eye Is on the Sparrow* she mentions her distrust of White people, though she worked with varieties of White entertainers and one of her closest letter writers was the writer and photographer Carl Van Vechten. However, race and racial entanglement in the evangelical world was thornier than in the world than the worlds of recording, stage, and Hollywood. Evangelicals held theological notions about forgiveness of sins and reconciliation.[68]

In addition, Waters wrestled deeply with her own personal flaws. In a series of letters to her secretary Floretta Howard she described her anger, angst, and frustrations. She wrote those letters using pious evangelical language describing her personal struggles ranging from fluctuating weight gain to love. She expressed vulnerability, remorse, and introspection. She frequently spoke of her need for forgiveness. She hoped that Jesus would help her to overcome negative behavior by defeating the devil in her. Waters wanted to be a part of a loving devotional community. However, what she never seemed to grasp was that devotional piety, though may be a beginning for personal or social change, was not sufficient. Her kind of piety would not change broader structures fueled by economics, laws, and politics that encased her individual life.[69]

The idea promoted by the Graham Crusade was that Christ had spiritually lifted the burden of race relationships through his atoning death on the cross for the forgiveness of each individual's sins. The sin of individual prejudices therefore was removed from the individual when he or she confessed and as a result reconciliation was made possible even across racial lines. The burden of evangelical theology required that Waters set aside her racial resentments, which she always struggled to do. It was highly problematic since structural inequalities were naively ignored by this untroubled way of believing.

On May 15, 1957, Waters staged her first appearances with Billy Graham's Crusade in New York City at Madison Square Garden. The revival lasted more than sixteen weeks and ended on September 1. Waters was there nightly, missing only one of the meetings. She was on stage when the Reverend Doctor Martin Luther King, Jr., made his only appearance with Graham at the Garden on July 18, 1957, to offer an invocation. King was also an impassioned American evangelical preacher with a revivalist mission. He offered a Black Social Gospel, a counter-narrative theology that prophetically challenged the nation as a whole to a different kind of morality, as opposed to the individuated doctrine that Graham preached. Recollecting his personal pilgrimage, exactly a year to the date that Graham ended his Madison Garden revival, King observed the following about his theological evolution:

Not until I entered Crozier Theological Seminary in 1948, however, did I begin a serious intellectual quest for a method to eliminate social evil. Although my major interest was in the fields of theology and philosophy, I spent a great deal of time reading the works of the great social philosophers. I came early to Walter Rauschenbusch's *Christianity and the Social Crisis*, which left an indelible imprint on my thinking by giving me a theological basis for the social concern which had already grown up in me as a result of my early experiences. . . . Rauschenbusch had done a great service for the Christian Church by insisting that the gospel deals with the whole man, not only his soul but his body; not only his spiritual well-being but his material well-being. It has been my conviction ever since reading Rauschenbusch that any religion, which professes to be concerned about the souls of men and is not concerned about the social and economic conditions that scar the soul, is a spiritually moribund religion only waiting for the day to be buried. It well has been said: "A religion that ends with the individual, ends."[70]

King's performance as revivalist emphasized national sins, not solely individual ones.[71] Like Waters and Graham, King was a masterful performer too;[72] his organization, the Southern Christian Leadership Conference (SCLC), was set on "redeeming the soul of the nation" in a different direction than Graham. Their differing emphases on what revival meant made King's and Graham's relationship, though respectful, an intellectually uneasy one.[73]

On May 17, two days after Graham's revival began in the Garden, King was leading his own in the District of Columbia. The Prayer Pilgrimage for Freedom was a social reform revival that used the commemorating of the United States Supreme Court's 1954 ruling on Brown v. Board of Education, which outlawed the Plessy v. Ferguson doctrine of separate but equal in schools and public accommodations, to push for stronger voter protections in the Southern states via a pending civil rights bill in Congress.[74] Appearing in his clerical robe, King stirringly addressed twenty-five to thirty thousand participants at the Lincoln Memorial in a public sermon titled "Give Us the Ballot."[75]

In spirit, Waters concurred with King's militancy. She understood racial oppression and humiliation well, and so throughout her show business career she engaged in civil rights activism as an entertainer by voluntarily performing at benefits to aid various causes and, of course, there was showstopping rendition of Suppertime. However, the practicalities of a show business life and her own needs as an aging woman forced her to lean toward Graham's version of evangelicalism rather than King's biblical militancy. SCLC's confrontational advocacy always made it difficult to pay the bills, even for King. Besides, SCLC had other superstar entertainers in their fold. And the beloved singer of King was the legendary "Queen of Gospel," Mahalia Jackson, who in 1963 made King extemporize about his dream at the Lincoln Memorial.

Waters therefore found a place within Graham Crusade, Inc. Her presence with the organization provided Graham with an integrationist cover, which in turn provided Waters with steady remuneration for an aging star's career. We must remember Waters had a triple burden. In Hollywood, she was Black, an aging woman, and a woman with ballooning weight and health difficulties. Though supremely talented, there was no room for her in a youth-obsessed industry. She was no longer vital, but she could be the setup person to bring the star of the show—Graham—to the stage. Waters's professional abilities to charmingly engage an audience with a testimony and her song "His Eye Is on the Sparrow" was perfect for Graham, who to his credit worked to racially integrate his crusades in the early 1950s. However, when Ethel Waters joined the crusade as a fading but bonafide star, she gave the Graham Crusades, Inc. even more legitimacy. Waters's appeal at the crusades allowed both White and especially Black believers to warm up to Graham's appeal that there was overall unity in Christ. In the contentiousness of the Civil Rights era, Waters's genial opening act signaled broadly that both moderate Blacks and Whites could trust him even though he was a religiously conservative, southern White man.

However, younger advocates did not see Waters's appearances with Graham the same way. They saw her performance as an embarrassing appeasement. The critics who indicted her reminded Waters of all the criticisms she had received in all phases of her career that did not conform to a politics of race-conscious respectability. Those criticisms stung Waters deeply. In 1950, years before joining the Graham crusade she had appeared on the television show *Beulah* and received harsh criticism within the Black Press for playing the role of a cheeky maid. Waters always felt that her middle-class critics, "the Dictys," did not understand that most entertainers were the hard-scrabbled Black poor and laboring classes like her. Entertainment was a vehicle of upward mobility and a way to feed a family. Hollywood never wrote fully developed and multifaceted Black characters, so actors had to creatively convey dignity through masterful comedy, jest, and performance. Black critics in Waters's mind wanted a kind of conformity that would have starved most Black actors and entertainers.

Later some Black artists, especially those inspired by the middle-class masculinity of jazz and the nationalist Black Arts Movement, viewed performers in the vein of Waters and Louis Armstrong as being too genial, too happy, and pejoratively minstrelsy. Her act did not reflect the movement. The irony of youthful critics like myself is that many of us were simply performing a different kind of Blackness ourselves, and defining that Blackness as the "only" way to be Black. What was hurtful to Waters about this was that we were the children of the "Dictys" trying to control her creativity in yet another fashion by critiquing her appearances with Graham.

I come full circle. Blackness as a cultural, political, and economic movement was transformative in my life. When I first saw Waters, I was interpreting her through the lens of my generation. The problem was I knew nothing of this woman's complexity or deep interiority. I passed quick judgment. I came of age amid the fervor of the Black Arts Movement and the male appeals of Black Power in the late 1960s and early 1970s. Histories, theologies, and philosophies grounded in Black experiences became an abiding intellectual passion for me. Waters legitimized Graham's efforts to be seen as "America's pastor."[76] Her performances welcomed Black folk to be persuaded that the evangelical fold was a safe one for them. And for a moment, through my high school years, I was swayed by the push of evangelicalism. In fact, there was an intersection of Black Power and American evangelicalism that has hardly been explored. In contrast, for an older generation, Waters's onstage performance out in front of Billy Graham was a powerful sign that a kind of utopian racial reconciliation might be a possibility.

However, Billy Graham's vision of American democracy was always a closed one. His ambitious religiously motivated agenda and political conservatism left a lot to be desired in terms of social justice for all Americans. Waters's performances with Graham played into an agenda that did not embrace the idea that queer Black believers such as herself could in fact name themselves among the "true believers." Though Ethel Waters's religious views were hardly orthodox, her work with Graham demanded that she stay firmly ensconced "in the closet." Although I came to disagree with her in a more mature way, I came to understand her faith, as well as class resentments more generationally in terms of survival and the need for respect and recognition. Graham's openness to her afforded her dignity and equality on an individual basis. Waters was never fraudulent about her faith. Her faith story in God allowed her to survive. It kept her "Heckle and Jekyll" personality attuned to a higher morality, a dignified humanity, guided by her prayers. She believed in something more powerful than herself even if it was tangled up with her competitiveness and drive. It gave her some impetus to take a risk and develop her musical talents as a professional show woman. Her leap of faith aided her escape from dire poverty with all its attendant personal hurts and sociological stratifications. She recognized that it was that transcendent quality called grace, not merely her superior skills and ambitions as an extraordinary performer that brought her to the highest levels of entertainment. Her faith kept her giving back to the Carmelite Monastery in Allentown, even as she crusaded with Graham. In retrospect, I have come to a deeper appreciation of Waters's glorious heterodoxies. She was not ashamed of who she was or whom she loved. She believed, she was proud, and she loved her people both publicly and privately. These were all acts of faith. Finally, however shrewd and staged it was for Waters to hitch her wagon to Graham, it too was an act of faith. In the end, she genuinely believed in a God that welcomed everyone and kept watch over all, even the sparrow.

# 2

# Jazz is her religion: Mary Lou Williams

It's spring, 1977, and I am a student at the University of Michigan. On September 1, five months later, Ethel Waters will die.[1] I am walking to what has quickly become one of my favorite stores, Ann Arbor's Schoolkids Records, just opened about nine months ago.[2] I am always eager to see new albums that were on display in the window or walk inside and hear an album spinning on the turntable. Schoolkids for me was a jazz lover's dream. The store banked on college students like me.

Jazz was in my estimation then Black intellectual music—Black high art music. I did not question my assumptions about what high art meant. I was not a fan of what I perceived as unwieldy improvisations or avant-garde—they seemed to me to have no "danceable Blues." Culturally, I was predisposed to see jazz as the domain of male instrumentalists—Duke, Basie, Bird, Dizzy, Louis, Miles, Tatum, and Trane. I did not have big ears gender wise; jazz was a masculine sound.[3] The exceptions were the exquisite vocals of Billie, Dinah, Ella, and Sarah.

A bit of background. I came of age years amid the hotly contested debates regarding schools of jazz. Throughout the late 1960s and early 1970s everything seemed up for grabs as music lovers asked a new question: Which jazz was "real" jazz? Some said it was established jazz musicians from the Swing and Bebop eras (1940s–60s), who were reaching younger and, in the main, White, audiences. Crossover groups like Weather Report (Wayne Shorter, Josef

Zawinul, and Jacob Pastorius) and Herbie Hancock bent "real" jazz in the direction of computerized electronic and "funk" beats, a direction dismissed by some jazz purists as watered-down music. "Hard Bop" as represented by the music of Art Blakey, Lou Donaldson, Eddie Harris, and others was played on jukeboxes in my childhood neighborhood, and blended jazz with Rhythm and Blues and Rock-n-Roll in its own form of "fusion." This was also true of the "Chicago Sound" characterized by artists as varied as Ramsey Lewis, Young Holt Unlimited and Earth, Wind, and Fire. The debate seemed endless.

Young college-age Black men like myself collected jazz albums to prove our intellectual bona fides. We were in a dialogue with our fathers and uncles, who had grown up as contemporaries to many of the great jazz artists to whom we were now listening. I was intent on building a jazz collection to rival one of my uncles in particular. For him, jazz represented male coolness, sophistication, and braininess. Representations on album covers of well-dressed men like the Modern Jazz Quartet reinforced a refined, urbane Black masculinity that we called coolness. Coolness was an epistemology, a way of knowing and analyzing the world around us and improvising responses and strategies to refashion it in our image.

There were other things on my mind that day I walked into Schoolkids. I had been thinking a great deal about jazz and religious faith. Could one be intellectual, cool, and faithful at the same time? Jazz musicians made claims to a variety of spiritualties rooted in many different world religions, but Protestant Christian evangelical sentiments seemed outside of that scope, viewed as square and unsophisticated. One notable exception was in 1958, when Duke Ellington and Mahalia Jackson collaborated on his Columbia LP *Black, Brown, and Beige*, melding her evocative gospel voice and lyrics with his jazz orchestration. It was a work fifteen years in the making. Then there was the trumpeter Donald Byrd's *1963 A New Perspective* that featured Black choral music. The penultimate paean to spirituality, though, was John Coltrane's *A Love Supreme*. Recorded at the end of 1964 and released as an album in February 1965, it became an instantaneous classic. Ten years after, when I began at Michigan, college students and other young people were still buying that album as though it was still hot off the press, and discussing it widely for its musical form and spiritual meaning.[4] With the release of *A Love Supreme*, jazz became not just intellectually cool, but deeply spiritual as well.

However, I knew nothing of Mary Lou Williams's music until I walked into Schoolkids. There I was enraptured listening to the vinyl entitled *Live at the Cookery* and its opening song, "Praise the Lord." I am held enrapt by her warm yet percussive playing, which, scholar Nicole Rustin keenly observes, has been too often compared to male musicianship.[5] Mary Lou as pianist and composer deserves more attention by scholars and music critics. The only thing I thought about her at the moment was that I wanted to hear more.

In 1977, I had no clue how much Mary Lou Williams's and Ethel Waters's lives were interconnected through their blackness, their gender, their entertainment professional status, and through their journeys to reconcile their inner lives through faith. Surely, I believed, there was a bit of providence in my encounter.

I would encounter Mary Lou Williams again in 2006–07 as a fellow of the National Humanities Center (NHC) in Research Park Triangle. Musicologist and Kenyon College professor of music Theodore E. Buehrer would also be a fellow that year too. Ted would spend his NHC year putting together a critical edition of Mary Lou's Big Band Compositions.[6] Here I came to understand the true majesty of her musical artisanship. And as a result of ongoing luncheon conversations with Ted, I began to think about her faith life and ponder what she thought about her religious journey. What did her journey of faith mean to her media and public interpreters? Did they understand it at all? Did they respect it?

When I began teaching at the University of Kansas in the fall of 2008, my friend and colleague professor Sherrie Tucker eagerly introduced me to another musicologist and professor of music Tammy Kernodle, who was one of Mary Lou's biographers. From that day in Schoolkids in 1977, I somehow had the feeling that Mary Lou and me were destined to connect.

# Becoming Mary Lou

Mary Lou Williams never became a larger-than-life celebrity like Ethel Waters, though she was a star. As a pianist and a composer, it was more difficult for Williams to be promoted in the same way as her more storied male counterparts. For Mary Lou, like Waters, music was a combination of talent, necessity, and finances. By all biographical accounts she was a prodigy. Early in life her prodigious talent for music was discovered when she would play back, on the piano, chords, and melodies by ear. Williams recalled, "I have been tied up with music for about as long as I can remember. By the time I was four I was picking out little tunes my mother played on the reed organ in the living-room." Her family allowed her talent to be groomed and cultivated. Her single mother took Mary Lou and moved from her birthplace Atlanta to Pittsburgh, to find both work and love in the industrial North.

Fighting poverty was the initial stage that Mary Lou played on. Mary Lou had been born before Franklin Delano Roosevelt's New Deal, when families struggled to keep their heads above water. Poverty silently assassinated thousands daily. Elites told themselves that it was "survival of the fittest." Being poor was viewed as a moral failing, especially if one were black and poor. To be a musical prodigy under the condition of poverty made it necessary for young Mary Lou to grow up fast as the eldest child and aid the family. So, music in her life was both a gift and a burden. The poet Langston Hughes's poem "Genius Child" expressed it plainly:

> This is a song for the genius child.
> Sing it softly, for the song is wild.
> Sing it softly as ever you can—
> Lest the song gets out of hand.
> *Nobody loves a genius child.*[7]

As a genius child, she had to navigate her musical talents and mature fast as a woman.

Mary Lou's family journey represented the raw material of Black life that the late August Wilson's used in his plays. These were the children that began life in Southern cities or born on plantations and small Midwest towns that migrated with their families to the industrial cities. They were the sons and daughters who came into adulthood, living and dying under the crushing weight of the Great Depression. They were also the ones who peered over the constant drudgery of day labor, the scant monetary rewards of domestic service, and the low-wage, dangerous, harrowing work of ditch-digging and in the foundries. Yet, daily they created and found spiritual uplift and unabashed joy in the music coming out of what the "high-saddity" called "disreputable places"—arcades, circuses, storefront churches, and gut bucket dives.

## "The Gigging Piano Girl from East Liberty"

Mary Lou's life was very much in keeping with the lives of her generation. She was from the less-than-glamorized side of the tracks. Her life was typical of the Black working poor. Mary Lou lived the Blues, being born in an era without a state-supported social safety net. Economically life was brutal for Black families, especially a girl child. Mary Lou was fortunate enough to be cocooned. Family meant a lot to the people of her generation despite economic insecurity and personal hurts. Family was strength—not the Victorian, bourgeois strength that centered around stable finances moored by fatherly control. Instead Black family revolved around bonds forged by external struggles and duty with all the ambivalences of familial love. The "little piano girl of East Liberty," as she was called in her community, began playing music because she had uncanny aptitude, and because she could add to her mother's meager earnings.

Mary Lou and her mother, Ginnie, struggled. Ginnie drank too much. She had been left by her children's father and was forced to rear Mary Lou and her sister alone. She controlled her daughters' behavior through physical discipline. However, Mary Lou was a particularly sensitive child and her physical punishments were crushing to her spirit rather than being lessons in self-control. She and her mother never aligned in their perceptions on physical discipline. As Mary Lou grew into her adolescent years, home became a burden, and she grew eager to flee her mother's harsh rule. She grew sullen and became disinterested in school. She daydreamed, infatuated by the excitement of what it might be like to be a high-paid pianist. Wisely her mother resisted her daughter's impulse. She was fearful that Mary Lou might be raped, molested, or have an unintended pregnancy that would drain more resources from their family if she played in theaters and clubs. And then there were the other things that could occur to a girl child. Would her daughter go missing and the police or sheriff never investigate it? Many times, law enforcement officials were perpetrators and culprits in the demise of young Black girls on the road. Lots of Black women were set up and served time in prison like their men folk, though it was spoken of in hushed whispers. The scenarios were numerous. The fears were real. And as Mary Lou stated, she looked older than her age at twelve. So, she and her mother had a test of wills, not simply because she drank too much and was a harsh disciplinarian, but because her mother dreaded what might happen to an adolescent entertaining in clubs. Some men were honorable, but there were enough sordid ones roaming in the dark to harm a young vulnerable woman. All this Mary Lou learned for herself after barely escaping an attack coming home one night in Pittsburgh.

The life Mary Lou's mother wanted for her was similar to what Ethel Waters's grandmother wanted for her daughters: middle-class respectability. Being a teacher in the Black world was an entree into middle-class status with its steady, but meager pay. It was certainly better than living in misery. Becoming a music teacher would provide her family a respectable status. However, the genius child felt compelled to leave home and play music on the open road.

Mary Lou's musical aptitude was initially cultivated through her experiences listening to and playing back music. When her mother discovered that she was gifted with musical recall, she did not want her to learn the conventions of music, fearing that a conventional music education would ruin Mary Lou's originality and voicing on the piano. Learning theory and notation would therefore come later. Regardless, Mary Lou's musical talents carried her to high and low places—from teas at the Andrew Carnegie's Mansion to joining the group Hits N' Bits on the road by the age of fourteen. In those days, the way to make a name was through the Black vaudeville circuit, predecessor to the "Chitlin Circuit" and dictated by Theater Owners' Booking Association, which Black performers called bitingly "Tough on Black Asses." Like many young people Mary Lou grew up dreaming of becoming a great performer with fame and riches.

Entertainment and performance for those talented enough or willing to work hard at performing have always lured genius children. It was a tempting, exciting path out of grinding poverty and the dysfunction and hurts of family. It was a way, so it appeared, to travel, make money, and build a stylish and lavish lifestyle. However, for those who dared, the occupation required long hours with little pay while moving from place to place, hoping for a break. It also required dealing with cheats and cutthroat theater owners who often refused to pay. And the competition was fierce whether trying out for a short stint in the circus, a popular tavern, or a big traveling show. In a highly stratified world where moneymaking defined one's social status, becoming a handsomely paid entertainer was like winning the mega-millions lottery. For many young people wishing to escape repressive and oppressive environments or who simply loved performing or both, it appeared to be an easier route to becoming well respected. But remember that it was just as difficult for a Black man or woman to become a successful physician or engineer or a union certified carpenter in those days; so, an entertainment career was just as reasonable a bet as being the community's local doctor. Mary Lou wagered that performing on the road would yield more than being a music teacher in a high school, a Pittsburgh industrial worker, or a mother. If she was going to have to work all of her life, she was going to do something that brought her gratification and perhaps a bit of glory. Playing to an adoring public was going to be her outlet to bring joy and receive love back in return.

# The piano has done well by me

When Mary Lou set out on her quixotic journey it was the thrills, the adventures, and the freedom that initially captured her. Though she was an extraordinarily talented young instrumentalist, she was not yet a musical professional and did not understand the American music industry. Being a talented pianist in a band was one thing; understanding music's legalities, corporate profit-making structures, and greedy managers was another. Young Mary Lou entered a business that ate the talented daily over a three-martini lunch; she was naïve to the business of entertainment. Her biographers, Linda Dahl and Tammy Kernodle, describe how she was initially paid in nice apparel and how her arrangements were co-opted under the bandleaders' name under whom she performed. This was the price of her ticket. It was a reminder of why Ethel Waters combatively and ruthlessly demanded the highest compensation.

Like Ethel Waters, Mary Lou had another exploitable asset: her body. Being on the road, she was always vulnerable to sexual harassment and assault. Women entertainers put themselves at great risk traveling with predominately male bands. Mary Lou, like her fellow pianist and contemporary Lil Hardin Armstrong, Louis Armstrong's second and arguably most influential wife, therefore chose to hitch their considerable talents to talented male musicians.[8] The context in which Hardin's and Williams's careers began was one guided by daily and routinized patriarchy; men breathe male dominance as they did air. The ideological subordination of girls and women was not given much reflection by men. It wasn't that the men surrounding Hardin or Mary Lou thought they were being patriarchal or sexist—they didn't. They simply took the differential status between men and women as natural. The entertainment world that jazz evolved in was simply a reflection of the multiple ways that women's lives were circumscribed. Even women of prodigious talent needed male patrons.

Mary Lou attached herself to John Williams, a superbly talented musician. Williams was an older man and initially guided her career and business affairs. And no doubt, he loved her and cherished his status as her protector. Williams was metaphorically Mary Lou's "beard," and she initially needed him and his wisdom out on the road. However, as she matured with self-understanding and professionally she realized that their relationship, though love existed between them, was a transactional one dictated by socially accepted male prerogatives. Williams, however, never wanted to give up being the dominant partner even when Mary Lou's star grew brighter and expanded. The arrangement they had as musicians and as a couple became unmanageable and discordant. She left him and went her own way.

Mary Lou left Pittsburgh in 1924 at the age of fourteen and lived a ceaseless performing life. Over her years on the road she discovered that making a living as a commercial musician and creating intricate and technically challenging compositions involved different strategies and obtained different rewards. The bands she performed in—Hits n' Bits, the Dark Clouds of Joy, and the Andy Kirk Orchestra—were commercial bands. They brought joy and release to the Black audiences whom they delighted. Their aesthetic required a danceable blues. These bands performed in front of audiences who faced day-to-day low-wage toil, daily public pronouncements of racial hatred, and an inner self-loathing that came from being portrayed as a national joke. These bands played melodies that accompanied the syncopated movement of feet, hips, and buttocks creating a loving space free of judgmental scorn. Mary Lou's initial road travel was exciting, promising fame, and perhaps wealth, but the night-after-night demands of performance grew weary and soulless. With twenty or more years on the road, Mary Lou had performed through the corporatization and consolidation of the recording industry, as well as the corporate consolidation of radio, and changes in copyright laws that favored composers and sheet music companies over performers and artists. Solely playing for commercial success was wearying, even when it involved playing in popular bands among appreciative Black audiences.

The world Mary Lou lived in had its grim sides and was filled with deathly inequalities. Nothing protected any Black person from the relentless humiliation and pressures of American apartheid. She and other musicians were able to bring infectious joy to the people for whom they performed. Mary Lou pursued a calling to creatively express herself through music, first as a gifted child and then as a professionally dedicated musical composer. Even before she was fully spiritually self-aware, in her self-fashioning she had found her calling in creating music.

# Elijah and the Juniper Tree

By the 1940s, Mary Lou had fulfilled her dream; she was a star, and settled in New York City. Those who heard her perform live and those who heard her over the radio airwaves appreciated her musicianship across the United States. Yet stardom, though enviable and seemingly glamorous, did not fulfill the voids in her life. By 1948, after twenty-four years of being on stage, Mary Lou was depleted. Her biographers note that this is the period when she attempted her first full jazz orchestral composition titled *Elijah and the Juniper Tree*. This is an interesting part of her musical career, crafting her composition around a story from the Hebrew Scriptures. Her biographers wrote from perspectives of music and musicology as opposed to religion and as a result missed an important aspect of Mary Lou's thinking about her own existential plight and faith journey.[9]

The biblical story of Elijah is the tale of a wearied prophet, worn down to a deathlike exhaustion. Mary Lou's Bible for this composition was the King James's version. She contemplated and composed Elijah's predicament against a backdrop of her own personal sufferings. She read herself into the Elijah story:

4   But he himself went a day's journey into the wilderness, and came and sat down under a juniper tree: and he requested for himself that he might die; and said, It is enough; now, O Lord, take away my life; for I am not better than my fathers.

5   And as he lay and slept under a juniper tree, behold, then an angel touched him, and said unto him, Arise and eat.

6   And he looked, and, behold, there was a cake baken on the coals, and a cruse of water at his head. And he did eat and drink, and laid him down again.

7   And the angel of the Lord came again the second time, and touched him, and said, Arise and eat; because the journey is too great for thee.

8   And he arose, and did eat and drink, and went in the strength of that meat forty days and forty nights unto Horeb the mount of God.

9   And he came thither unto a cave, and lodged there; and, behold, the word of the Lord came to him, and he said unto him, What doest thou here, Elijah?

10  And he said, I have been very jealous for the Lord God of hosts: for the children of Israel have forsaken thy covenant, thrown down thine altars, and slain thy prophets with the sword; and I, even I only, am left; and they seek my life, to take it away.[10]

Mary Lou fully related to Elijah's story, one she no doubt had heard vividly, retold and reformulated by Black preachers. The prophet's exhaustive woe was her story, one she felt needed a jazz composition to add to the bevy of renditions. Mary Lou, like Elijah, was in need of rest. She was no longer an adolescent; she had come into her full power as a featured pianist having toured the country. It was time for a rest and she sought her family's home. Her return to Pittsburgh was not a respite. It was no sabbatical reprieve. Instead her family members abused her reliable financial support with charges from stores without her permission even though she was not working. In her mother's house, she found no relief, nor the loving acceptance or the emotional space she sought. What she found instead was the greedy consumptive desires and demands of family. They viewed Mary Lou's artistic acclaim as a source of unlimited wealth. She had returned home to find a sense of peace, but peace was elusive.

Other more private matters wore her down too. This female counterpart of Elijah was utterly worn down by her frequent and constant performances. She may not have vanquished Yahweh's defilers, but she had performed for his chosen night after night. And then there was the most of secretive of matters: her abortion. She had chosen her musical career over being a single mother. Music was her baby. She was no different than Duke Ellington who titled his memoir *Music is My Mistress*, which the tag line read, "Music is my mistress, and she plays second fiddle to no one."[11] However, unlike Ellington, a man whose former wife, Edna Thompson Ellington, took care of their only son Mercer as he traveled the globe, Mary Lou did not have that kind of support system. She was the caretaker of her family and herself. Even though her circumstances may have justified her action, she nevertheless was full of self-reproach about her decision. Her guilt did not dissipate; she was remorseful for decades, perhaps the remainder of her life, as she later confessed to her agent and Catholic priest Father Peter O'Brien. In addition, she was tired of trying to make commercially inspired music for mass appeal, and fatigued by her insatiably needy family.

Mary Lou's *Elijah and the Juniper Tree* was more than an experiment in composition. She was storying, trying to make some sense of her own inner life and commitments. She would be years away from fully describing her inner life in specifically Catholic terms, but this composition was a part of the process of figuring out her own story. *Elijah and the Juniper Tree* was a leap of faith as much as it was a composition. It was her foray into reconciling her own existential crisis. Nineteenth-century Danish philosopher Soren Kierkegaard would have understood her wrestling perfectly.

Perhaps as her biographers have argued, Mary Lou's *Elijah and the Juniper Tree* missed the mark as a musical composition. Yet looking back on her life from the perspective of an inner history, she was amid her own spiritual journey and this particular orchestration signaled it. Mary Lou's inner history had two major narrative streams flowing out and into each other. The first was her cultural foundation from Black Protestantism. She simply learned to play music in the spaces that Black Americans created, those religious congregations and organizations that daily touched and interacted with everyday Black folk for good or ill. That stream gave her biblically inspired hymnody, an Old Testament (Hebrew Scripture) storytelling, the Negro spirituals, the evolution of the gospel blues among Black Pentecostals and Baptists, and musically intoned chanted sermons. Mary Lou's growing up years were fashioned by the liturgical inventiveness that took place in Black Protestant spaces. Her initial language of faith that included her musicality was honed by the everydayness of Black worshipping rituals that bandaged the daily cuts that disfigured Black Americans, daily cuts that she and Ethel Waters shared.

The second stream, which intertwined with the first, was found globally in mysticism and spiritual logics.[12] It is believed that children born with a "caul" have a special power to see beyond the living.[13] Mary Lou was delivered with a caul, a thin fetal membrane that covers the body of the infant and is said to give the child the ability to see the dead or second sight to see the future.[14] Ideas about a caul had long resonated in West African explanations of the world, particularly within the Ashanti nation of Ghana. In the era of chattel slavery in the United States, southern White masters and planters generally dismissed these spiritual claims as yet another Black American superstition, but the belief that a caul had spiritual power persisted. The eminent historian and sociologist W. E. B. DuBois referenced the caul as "the veil" in his tour de force *Souls of Black Folk*.[15] He flipped the idea into a sociological description. That is, Black Americans were able to see things about power and inequality that other Americans missed. But Mary Lou's caul remained spiritual. It was a troublesome second sight that interacted with the living and dead. All around her were presences of people long gone. For a musician traveling on the road staying in rooming houses, hotels, and homes, having the ability to see the living and dead was vexatious. In many of these spaces there were troubling incidents that occurred—murders, untimely deaths of children, and suicides. If she could see behind the veil then she was witness to both goodness and the unresolved hauntings of the spirits who looked to rest. This meant that Mary Lou was attuned to a spirit world and it informed her musical intellect. Her mystical encounter with nonmaterial reality fit into a Black cosmological world out of which grew Black Protestantism itself.

Culture critic Farah Jasmine Griffin's book *Harlem Nocturne: Women Artists & Progressive Politics During World War II* is a fabulous incursion into the rich contributions of Black women artists in the era of the Second World War. Griffin writes of Mary Lou as a mature and well-regarded pianist performing at New York's Café Society, an emerging composer, and an intellectual leader facilitating bebop and jazz composition. She explores Mary Lou's accomplishments and pitfalls as she expands herself as a woman and artist. And Griffin was correct to redress omissions by jazz musicians, critics, and historians alike who failed to engage her artistry! In this era of Mary Lou's life, she was intellectually expansive, and musically an intellectual mentor, one whose thought and work emerges out of a deep sense of struggle with her own inner journey. Here I find myself wondering why Griffin did not connect this critical aspect of her life to her intellectual creativity. It is precisely in this period that she is also wrestling with questions of transcendence, ritual, and the need for forgiveness, love, and meaningful companionship. Griffin beautifully observes that *Mary Lou Williams: The Circle Recordings*, recorded in 1951 and released posthumously in 2006, "is like listening to a sonic autobiography."[16] My argument with Griffin is that her music in these recordings was derived from a spiritual wrestling that she would later scaffold into her religious commitment. Her sonic autobiography was not separated in a Cartesian-like fashion, a separation of her mind from her body. Mary Lou was always spiritually seeking, in search of a holism. In fact, Griffin observes that Mary Lou "had a long-standing interest in the zodiac." She writes:

> At this stage in her life she hungered for spiritual meaning and guidance, but she did not have a sense of religiosity. For her, music was a spiritual medium, a conduit to something outside of herself as well as a vehicle for expressing a sense of the spiritual, if not the divine. She operated in a secular world, that of jazz and show business, yet the jazz world was nonetheless characterized by its own expression of the spirit.[17]

Griffin offers a useful explanation, but we differ. Mary Lou did have a sense of religiosity. It was born of Black Protestantism. Her fascination with astrology was not atypical of what religious scholar Henry H. Mitchell termed "Black Belief" in 1975.[18] In Black communities, Mitchell argued beliefs are set side by side with each other and are judged on how efficacious they are in practice for living a good life. Astrology was a means, and has always been one, for people to organize the universe and explain personality traits. In 1971, English historian Keith Thomas wrote a richly researched book titled *Religion and the Decline of Magic* that argued that medieval Englanders sought multiple ways explaining and coping with daily sufferings and maladies outside and inside the Roman Catholic Church. Ordinary folk used popular beliefs such as astrology, divinations, ghost, and fairies, as well as the cult of the saints. Thomas's argument was that European Protestants sought to undermine Catholic theological claims for what they believed was a truer form of Christianity, a biblically based one. These religious protesters would use a kind of biblical rationalism that would eventually open the way for a new form of scientific rationalism. The magical world would soon be replaced by a kind of secular rationality that would subdue the mystical. There is no doubt that Thomas's insights are profound, and expressed aspects of a truth, but if we insert instead the beliefs of Black descendants of the transatlantic slave trade and other persons of color in the diaspora, we might find that even with the rise of Euro-Protestant and scientific rationalism, counter explanations never went away among the world's people. If the writer had understood Mary Lou's community, he might have conceded that science, religion, and "superstitions" all lived together and are demarcated by utility, expediency, healing, and hopefulness.[19]

In 1945, Mary Lou's jazz orchestration titled *The Zodiac Suite* was in keeping with efficacious Black belief. It was congruent with her interest in trying to find enduring goodness or explanatory power in a maddening world of global war. Her interest in the zodiac was linked to being born with a caul, as well as the Black Protestantism that culturally formed her. Her difficulty with Black Protestantism was that it had no specific ways of addressing the other dimensions of Black life. Its mix with White evangelical Biblicism provided no organized answers and simplistically reduced the universe's pluralism to a formulaic and rigid faith. It would have been interesting if she had encountered the theologian Howard Thurman in this period. Mary Lou could see things, and her faith helped her to meaningfully organize the things she saw among both the living and the dead.

For Mary Lou's inner history, *Elijah and the Juniper Tree* was a moment of questioning and faith consciousness. Just what kind of faith did she wish to possess? What were her aspirations? What was her spiritual calling to serve? How could she demonstrate love and justice through musicianship? She sat under her own juniper tree. The composition eerily foreshadowed her ten years full of dreadful nights struggling against loneliness, taming her gambling addiction, and rebuilding her poor finances. Serendipitously, she composed this at the same time that Thomas Merton, the aesthete critic turned Marxist, found self-meaning in a Trappist Monastery and released his best-selling memoir *Seven Story Mountain*. His 1948 memoir told a story of an end to spiritual weariness, and of freedom. Merton's journey from modern weariness to solitude and brotherhood was compelling. In that solitude, he found freedom in God. Following Merton's lead, Mary Lou began her tortuous crossing to organize her conflicting ideal of herself in the spiritual home of Roman Catholicism.

# The prayerful one

Even though Mary Lou became a Roman Catholic, her foundational religious culture, if not beliefs, had been shaped by Black Protestantism. She had been nurtured in a tradition that was influenced by the European Reformation that emphasized the Protestant Bible as the exclusive text for defining Christianity. The English version of the Protestant Bible, known as the *King James Version*, was frequently read aloud and deeply influenced the lives of countless slaves born in the United States. It was to gain deep resonance with their desire to be free, and it found a home in evangelical formulations of Christianity—Baptist and Methodist—that gave the utmost regard to the individual personhood before God. This adopting of the Bible and Evangelicalism, combined with the many cultural importations of African societies, created a new world Christianity and became a Protestantism that was stitched, weaved, and quilted in ways that the people who held court in sixteenth-century Switzerland, such as Ulrich Zwingli and Jean Calvin, could never have anticipated. Slave preachers and their invisible churches refashioned Protestantism musically through songs of freedom, labor, and sorrow. Those songs were theology, as Howard Thurman has pointed out.[20] The enduring tentacles of chattel slavery restricted printed scholastic theology by banning the enslaved from the written Word, and forced that Word instead to be sung and embodied in dance. Its subjects were life and death, hope and despair about a mighty Hebrew Jesus who faced woeful conditions and unjust punishments, and used God's power to provide freedom and forgiveness. The liturgy, the highly stylized work of worshipping, was done in myriad ways given Southern regionalism and was sourced from multiple influences of Atlantic societies from Africa to Europe. Mary Lou's very own percussive piano style emerged from her initial engagement in Black Protestant culture.

Though Mary Lou's life emerged in Black Protestantism, it did not mean that foundation fulfilled her inward desires. One of the greatest things about mass Black urbanization, which historians call the Great Migration, was that it provided freedoms both personal and political. It was plain: looking back on Mary Lou's life in terms of her lived experiences, we clearly see that her formative tradition had run dry. Her years on the road and then making her home in New York had exposed to her too much intellectually to be a pliant, conventional believer. Her consistent performing in New York's Café Society had put her in regular contact with Jews, Marxists, agnostics, and atheists. Walking down the streets of Harlem alone, she recognized that there were multiple expressions of faith occurring simultaneously: Black Baptist, Hebrew, Holiness, Methodist, Muslim, Pentecostal, and so many other religions. Yet she was drawn to Catholicism like a growing number of Black folk who had left their communities of origin whether in the American South or the West Indies.

Mary Lou was not the only Black American artist to find some solace in Catholicism. In his waning years of life, writer Claude McKay of Harlem Renaissance fame also found a grace space in Catholicism. After his most productive years of writing success, McKay found illness and other creative roadblocks stalling a once-promising career. Catholic workers literally nursed him back to health. He, like many, found Catholic novena important in his troubled life before he died.[21]

And though small in number relative to Black Protestants, early Black Catholics were strategically positioned in important cities like Baltimore, New Orleans, and along the Gulf Coast. From the 1920s onward tiny Black parishes congealed slowly around the country from Chicago to Detroit to New York.[22] And slowly American Catholic Bishops began recognizing that their schools could minister and evangelize new urban migrants. The greatest difficulty was that there were too few Black priests. American-style racism inflecting within Catholic Church made desegregation of the altar a difficult fight.[23] Nevertheless, there were faithful on the move seeking religious alternatives from the ones that shaped them; they searched for what they considered was a more expansive spirituality.[24] New converts like McKay and Mary Lou joined with the small number of cradle Black Catholics who built and sustained parishes and institutions.[25] "By 1957, New York City had the third largest African-American Catholic community with 57,000 members. It followed Lafayette, Louisiana that had 75,000 black Catholics and New Orleans that had 71,000 black Catholics."[26]

Though Mary Lou visited churches like Harlem's Abyssinian Baptist Church, she held an anti-Black clericalism. Her limited exposure to Black churches made her leery of the charismatic leadership of the Black clergy. She did not know whether to trust Black clerics as hustlers or spiritual leaders. Her views reflected the average skepticism that could be heard on the streets in urban Black communities in the United States. Were preachers raising the money for the mission of the church or for their own benefit? Lastly, the doors of the church were closed except for designated meetings of the congregation. The limitations of Black congregations served as a disincentive for Mary Lou receiving nurture in her time of crisis. In contrast, Harlem's Our Lady of Lourdes was never closed for prayer.[27]

By the early 1950s, Mary Lou was in crisis. She moved to Europe, attempting to find the autonomy to compose less commercial music while earning steady wages. Mary Lou hoped to take advantage of the post-Second World War, Cold War–era cultural cache that evolved around jazz as a democratic musical form.[28] But moving to England and France proved equally as wearisome as it had been in the United States. There was no quick money to be made, no residency that provided creative freedom or freedom from her own consumerism. Mary Lou's dissonant self, sailed along with her across the ocean.

According to Mary Lou's biographers it was in this period that she began contemplating writing an autobiographical memoir. I have no empirical evidence, simply a hunch, given the time period and the wide publicity—Waters's 1951 memoir *His Eye Is on the Sparrow* spurred her writing pursuits. After all, Waters represented a woman's spiritual journey in the entertainment business that was akin to her own. I cannot help but think that Waters's long-celebrated career and publishing success was in the back of Mary Lou's mind as she sought out a publisher and a cowriter for a memoir.[29] As Linda Dahl points out at the beginning of her biography, the journeys of Mary Lou, Billie Holiday, and Ethel Waters were similar in their struggles as Black women artists. Though widely loved in Black communities, Mary Lou never reached popular superstardom or crossover status as the indefatigable Waters, nor did she have a tale of self-destructiveness as dramatic as Holiday's. Duke Ellington, Count Basie, and host of rising male stars such as Thelonious Monk overshadowed her in popularity as jazz pianists and composers. Magazines such as *Down Beat* and *Playboy* were male-centric and in theory offered a "race neutral" approach to jazz criticism and promotions.[30] To put it bluntly, the recording industry simply favored men as "genius" composers and instrumentalists. A memoir written by Mary Lou, though interesting would not have had as wide of an audience as Waters's unless she embellished it. But she would never portray her life in the manner that William Duffy fictively sensationalized the life of Billie Holiday in *Lady Sings the Blues* in 1956.[31] Mary Lou was far more scrupulous and caring. She would not exaggerate the woes of her family or jazz musicians who were also her family. It would have made good business sense to play up the stereotype of jazz musicians as hipsters and drug addicted, but she refused to betray her friends. Her story would have to be told a different way. She would have to settle for a less lucrative way than a book contract for conveying her journey of faith and artistry. She would serialize her story in interviews. She began with the English jazz magazine *Melody Makers*, and pursued other write-ups in newspapers and magazines.

The autobiography was never completed. By 1954, Mary Lou's stress was at breaking point and she returned back home and dropped out of performing.

Mary Lou would find a great Catholic ally in Thomas Merton. Merton's 1948 best-selling memoir *Seven Story Mountain* recollected his Catholic conversion. He describes his life as an upper-class child traveling with his father to the great historical sites and cathedrals of Europe, followed by his years at Columbia University studying literature with initial aspirations to be a literary critic, his foregoing literature for revolution struggle as a Communist, and then at age twenty-six finding his true vocation as a Trappist monk.[32] Here was an aesthete-turned-activist who then removes himself from public and turns to a life of cloistered contemplation. Here was a book that spoke to her own struggle of trying to make sense of her own need for God and the greater meaning of her jazz artistry. Like Merton, Mary Lou found it necessary to cloister herself for a time too.

In 1956, Mary Lou cloistered herself and halted public performances. Interestingly enough, it was the same year that Merton wrote another book that perhaps spoke to her interior search for stability titled *The Living Bread*. Merton argued that at the center of Christian life was the Eucharist. Ritual partaking of communion was at center of human beings' mystical relationship to Christ. The *Living Bread* is one of Merton's more conservative books. By conservative I mean that Merton framed his argument within the bounds of Cold War rhetoric of anticommunism and his reinforcement of the Catholic Church's patriarchal leadership, with males the only proper priests and bishops. Nevertheless, given the time period, Merton's words resonated for Mary Lou:

Love for God is the deepest fulfillment of the powers implanted by God in our human nature which He was destined for union with Himself. In loving Him, we discover not only the inner meaning of truth which we would otherwise never be able to understand, but we also find our true selves in Him. The charity which is stirred up in our hearts by the Spirit of Christ acting in the depths of our being makes us begin to be the persons He has destined us to be in the inscrutable designs of His Providence. Moved by grace of Christ we begin to discover and to know Christ Himself as a friend knows a friend—by the inner sympathy and understanding friendship alone can impart. This loving knowledge of God is one of the most important fruits of Eucharistic communion with God in Christ.[33]

As Mary Lou began to translate her life as a Catholic, her understanding of the Eucharist as mystical sacrifice was "something more than a prayer of pardon" as Merton claimed. She, in all probability, understood his observation that "each time the Mass is offered, the fruits of our Redemption are poured out anew upon our souls." As her crisis years came to resolution, she found a guiding light in a communal understanding of the Mass, ideas that she would later incorporate into her composition and performance. Merton wrote that "by uniting ourselves with the sacred rite of the Mass and above all by receiving Holy Communion, we enter into the sacrifice of Christ. We mystically die with the divine Victim and rise again with Him to a new life in God." He continued, "We are freed from our sins and we are once again pleasing to God," "and we receive grace to follow Him more generously in the life of charity and fraternal union which is the life of His Mystical Body."[34] And there is no doubt she felt freer. Mary Lou in a replay of the Augustinian autobiographical tradition turned her focus away from herself, away from her own personal frustrations and woes, and toward seeing more clearly the needs of others.[35]

By 1956, Mary Lou was living an ascetic existence as her biographer Tammy Kernodle describes. She perhaps knowingly followed Merton's path without joining a monastery. She gave up material goods, invited a poor family to live with her, washed their clothes and provided for them even when she did not have money coming herself. Her sense of conversion was so present to Mary Lou that it disturbed her friends. Kernodle writes:

Those who witnessed Mary's transformation tried to adjust. Her conversations, which were once full of stories of the jazz scene or of the newest musical development, were now centered on the discussions of God, the fate of humanity, and the need for everyone to pray. Some musicians and friends avoided her as much as possible, unable to withstand the "sermons" she was certain to launch into and saddened by her physical deterioration. According to her niece, "She was like a bag lady—not crazy, but odd, running here and there with bags of groceries, trying to help these strung-out musicians.[36]

On May 9, 1957, Father Anthony Woods baptized Mary Lou at Our Lady of Lourdes in Harlem as a fully communicant member of the Christian Church. Her baptism was not insignificant. For Mary Lou, she was a new person. This ancient practice aligned her self-values with Christ-informed values. Her baptism indicated that she had turned her life over to the Catholic Church's ethical and spiritual guidance. The church claimed the central place in her life and would guide her behavior and community. As a result of her new-found Catholic faith, she prayed for and with her fellow jazz musicians. Prayer and devotion became central to her life.[37]

It took a couple of years for Mary Lou to find her spiritual balance as a Catholic convert. Through the assistance of Fathers John Crowley and Anthony Woods she found her way back to being a jazz performer. They aided her in gaining perspective about the spiritual usages of her talents. And it is noteworthy that the irrepressible jazz innovator and trumpeter Dizzy Gillespie encouraged her to return to public performances. Through these supports and guidance, she found her way back to the stage. A purposeful lay ministry guided her stage performances. Her own charity, the Bel Canto Foundation, formed to service the jazz community, caught up in the widespread urban heroin epidemic. Musicians, writers, and enthusiastic fans had believed the mistaken notion that the opiate might enhance their performance or relieve them from stress. Instead, these people along with ordinary people around Harlem and the Greenwich Village found themselves addicted to the sleep-inducing drug. The addiction was rampant and created community desperation from the creative class to the lower classes.

Though Mary Lou found inner contentment and purposefulness in her Catholicism, it would not render her blind to being a Black Catholic in the United States. While she aligned her life with orthodoxy of the Eucharistic theology as Merton described, Mary Lou's life as Black American was in fact a form of heterodoxy. In Catholic theology orthodoxy means "right practice" or "right praise," meaning the openness of spirit and ritual obeisance was bound by the church's authoritative teachings. This was conflictual on a number of fronts. It goes without saying that Black Catholics were shaped by the ethos of Black Protestants. This ethos questioned hierarchy. However, more importantly, this ethos places great emphasis on the freedom of conscience, as a Christian virtue over obedience. It was an unspoken and abiding rule within Black communities. Harriet Beecher Stowe, for all her mistaken notion about slaves and slavery, got Uncle Tom's inner conscience correct. Black Protestant culture had taught succeeding generations to follow the primacy of one's own conscience as the most important aspect of one's inner freedom. Slavery's natal alienation created a faith-based dialectical response to social conformity that was expressed by freedom of conscience.[38] Mary Lou's life as a woman, a well-traveled musician traversing through both racial apartheid and sexist exclusion, had built-in ready-made conflicts with Catholic orthodoxy. If Mary Lou were to live as a faithful Catholic she would have to Blacken the faith. This meant that her orthodoxy had to lead to justice or "righteous praise."

Music scholar Gayle Murchison aptly contextualizes Mary Lou's Catholic catechesis amid a civil rights revolution. If Mary Lou was being catechized and baptized, so too was the United States. Civil Rights resisters were catechizing the nation away from a White racial democracy toward an inclusive democracy. *Brown v. Board of Education*, the terrorist murder of Emmett Till, the Montgomery Bus Boycott in Alabama, and nine young souls in Little Rock had galvanized Black communities both in the South and the North and baptized the country in a movement of national resistance.[39] Mary Lou always had inchoate and resentful political sentiments about American racial injustice. As a prominent Black member in a road band, she lived and ate Jim Crow from one show to the next. However, she cultivated a broader sense of self politically in her years performing at Café Society in New York City's Greenwich Village. It should be remembered that New York was one of the Civil Rights Movement's most important epicenters.[40]

From 1938, when Barney Josephson founded Café Society, until the late 1940s when it was shut down, the club was a magnet for openness, cultural activism, and social causes, and more importantly jazz, especially for Black women artists. The who's who list for the club is too lengthy to enumerate. Suffice it to say that Billie Holiday's recording of the poem *Strange Fruit* about southern lynching was first sung in Josephson's club. The club was a hub of cultural and political exchange and Mary Lou intellectually grew amid these exchanges. These lessons corresponded with the ones she grew up with and faced incessantly on the road. In Mary Lou's words "the race" made her political interactions at club sharper, but at heart she was a musician.

> Yes, I got hung up in it through working in the Cafe [i.e., Café Society], but I think all musicians or people like me would get mixed up in something, looking for some people to help them and help the race. But they can never be anything but a musician. Through doing benefits and a lot of other things, and you don't know how serious it is—but there's not one musician I think would be in any kind of political anything if they weren't disturbed about the race, as being abused and whatnot of the race, trying to help the poor. I've been in practically everything.[41]

Being a Black Catholic, Mary Lou could not give up the political struggles of "the race." As Father Anthony Woods knew, racism and discriminatory practices were a part of the church, its American Bishopric, and justified by early modern Papal ratifications. The Papal endorsements or "bulls of discovery" were justifications to give Portuguese and Spanish monarchies spheres of influence in the non-European world. The merchant-militarized classes of these kingdoms—sailors, pirates, and conquistadores—conveniently found these statements morally useful in establishing trade in minerals, agricultural produce, and eventually human beings. These persons acting on behalf of the state with doctrinal confirmation bound indigenous peoples of Africa and South America and forcibly categorized them into slaves, servants, and, worse, the ethnically cleansed. This was the precise substance of Peter Claver and Martin de Porres's biographies living in Spanish-colonized Columbia and Peru, respectively. Their mission ministries were carried out in a world with the rancid saltwater smell of slave ships, the slave markets of Cartagena to Lima, and the stench of indigenous bodies overworked and dying in the mines in colonies throughout South America. There was a political urgency surrounding each man's canonization in 1888 and 1962, respectively. Brazilian abolition of slavery in 1888, and African independence movements and the United States civil rights revolution in the late 1950s and 1960s, provided the rationale for each canonization. These outside events forced Popes Leo XIII and John XXIII, respectively, to alter their spiritual prelates' precedents. The church's princes, the Cardinals, found it necessary to rethink and mute Rome's role as an important factor in the early modernist brutality of slavery.

No Catholic catechesis is expected to know such a history and Mary Lou was not fully aware of all its specificities. What she was aware of was that St. Martin de Porres was Black (mixed-race) and lived amid a slaveholding society, and like her he suffered racial injustices, yet he nevertheless found healing powers that benefited others. He was a role model of charity, the deepest expression of self-giving humanity. In June 1962, she began composing *St. Martin de Porres*, which would be eventually recorded on her 1964 album titled the *Black Christ of the Andes*. Mary Lou as a musician was moving into new territory composing jazz arrangements for a liturgical setting.[42] This part of her music spoke to her new realities as a Catholic. She was bringing a form of music that had arisen from dancehalls, brothels, juke joints, the theater, and circuses—places and spaces of disreputable reputations. Here was a world music born in places of ignobility, where suffering was everyday life. From these lowly quarters were derived the Blues, a blues with a "healing and love in the music."[43] She viewed the origins of jazz as derived from the anguish of American slavery. Her thoughts echoed Howard Thurman and W. E. B. DuBois:

> From suffering came the Negro spirituals, songs of joy, and songs of sorrow. The main origin of American Jazz is spiritual. Because of the deeply religious background of the American Negro, he was able to mix this strong influence with the rhythms that reached deep into the inner self to give expression to outcries of sincere joy, which became known as Jazz.[44]

As Murchison cites, Mary Lou viewed jazz as a spiritually informed music that was rooted in the Black American's long journey to find spiritual and legal emancipation. However, most Catholic and Protestants alike viewed jazz as well as variations of the blues to be dangerous to right living. Western European doctrinal ethics, the varieties of church teachings, had always tried to place a buffer between the sacred and the profane. Jazz's origin and the music's sexual connation caused the Catholic hierarchy to look askance at a form of music derived from the experiences of a despised subgroup in the United States.

In contrast, the Black Americans' for bears who arrived on the shores of the Americas had no notions of the sacred or the profane. These varied people viewed the world as embodied of both good and bad behavior that manifested in human beings, gods, and the ancestors alike. Therefore music, like so many other things that humans manipulated and embodied, contained forms that could be used for either goodness or badness depending on the occasion and the intent. In point of fact, the Blues were liturgically performed in many Black Urban Protestant congregations in both the North and the South. By the time Mary Lou composed *St. Martin de Porres* to express her new-found

Catholic sensibilities, Black Protestants had used their music to reshape the voicing of US popular music.

This ever-widening scope of the Gospel Blues, led by Black Protestant southern migrants like Thomas Dorsey and a bevy of Black women church musicians such as Chicago's Mahalia Jackson, Sallie Martin, and Willie Mae Ford Smith, was an underground revolution. Their performing venues ranged from urban congregations to concert halls. They composed a commercial music that spoke to the spiritual demands of a Black Southern diaspora spreading across the United States. In 1958, as Mary Lou was trying to figure out how to direct her life and art as a Catholic, Duke Ellington was musically collaborating with Mahalia Jackson in the recording of *Come Sunday* on the recording of his suite *Black, Brown, and Beige*. Hard Bop, jazz that encompassed variations of the blues including Gospel, R&B, and dynamic percussion led by Art Blakey and the Jazz Messengers featured such songs as *Moanin*, signifying the spiritual rhythms of Black church folk. It is within this context that Mary Lou began her musical theologizing.

Mary Lou was not the only jazz musician attempting to make her inner logic cohere through religion or spirituality at the time of her Catholic conversion. A number of musicians found it necessary to locate themselves within organized faith communities—Baha'i, Buddhist, Christian, and Muslim—in an effort to make sense of the exigencies of history and self-struggles.[45] Mary Lou was an important member of the wider jazz community, openly expressing her artistry and her dependency on a faith that she viewed as expanding her personhood by being selfless as Christ. She joined musicians recording spiritually and religiously intoned pieces and albums such as trumpeter Donald Byrd's 1963 *A New Perspective*, John Coltrane's 1965 *A Love Supreme*, and Duke Ellington's *A Concert of Sacred Music*.

All the while, Mary Lou attempted to help the Catholic hierarchy understand the liturgical uses of jazz. She had moved to impact Catholic/Christian theology in recording the album *Black Christ of the Andes*. Father

Peter O'Brian, her late manager, observes that "Williams, in placing *Black* and *Christ* together in one electrifying phrase *Black Christ*, unified her own religious belief with the political struggle of the period. This album is the statement of her intertwined beliefs about faith in God, faith in black people, faith in America, and faith in jazz."[46] Her composition blackened Catholicism theologically through jazz voicing by uplifting the voices of the racialized and the poor descendants of the transatlantic slave trade all throughout the Americas. Mary Lou's 1963 recording of *St. Martin de Porres* for her album *Black Christ of the Andes* was as much pious as it was a revolutionary act. She foreshadowed the 1968 Conference of Latin American Bishops, which birthed Catholic Liberation Theology and James Cones in 1969 prophesying *Black Theology, Black Power*. And I have to believe St. Martin de Porres and Martin Luther King, Jr., were kindred spirits in her mind. As Father O'Brien observes, *Black Christ of the Andes* was equally musical offering to Catholic Church and a statement in support of the ongoing political protest of the Movement.

As important as her recording of *Black Christ of the Andes* was a jazz expression of faith, Mary Lou was not willing to concede blues to free jazz, the form launched by saxophonist Ornette Coleman. In *Time* magazine, she responded to the reporter "Have you heard these 'freedom players?' . . .They're making people sick all over town." By contrast, she thought of "herself as a 'soul' player" in the melodic and blues idiom. "'I am praying through my fingers when I play'. . . 'I get that good 'soul sound,' and I try to touch people's spirits."[47]

Mary Lou failed to convince the Catholic prelates as to the importance of jazz's soul sound even after Vatican II, the Church Council that permitted vernacular and cultural idioms into the mass. Even a brief audience with Pope Paul VI could not persuade the Vatican bureaucracy that a jazz mass should be used in worship before His Holiness. The provincially European-led Roman Catholic Church was not welcoming of her mass, a music that sprang from exploitative toil and peasantry. Nevertheless, her music stirred more than a few Catholics in the United States and in Africa. Her mass, which was intended to be used at the Vatican, was instead used in the memorialization of Tom Mboya, Kenyan labor unionist, global activist, and Catholic who was assassinated in 1969. It was titled *Mass for Peace*. Her failed attempt at the Vatican could not suppress her musical statement of faith in which she expressed the long-suffering hopes of oppressed people for peace and justice. She was way ahead of the Catholic episcopacy, as everyday believers often are. Her jazz mass with its theological valorization of Black struggle challenged the quotidian pastoral pacification to engage in a peaceful struggle for equality.

## Jazz is her religion

By the 1970, Mary Lou had made peace with herself as a jazz musician informed by her Catholic spirituality. Her handbill flyer for her concert made clear her understanding:

JAZZ

is your heritage—born—of the
suffering of the early American
Black people—the only true
American art form—it is
spiritual and healing to the
Soul—Listen with the ears
of your heart and go home
healed—keep jazz alive
call your favorite
TV-radio stations
and record
stores
NOW

By then Mary Lou had found a fuller voice, countering all the sociological ghettoization theorization about the permanence of weakness and failures of Blackness. She was joyfully collaborating with the Alvin Ailey Dancers who rendered her *Mass for Peace* into a visually arresting modern dance. She asserted it was necessary for Black Americans "to realize their own importance." Black people are, she opined, "the most inventive, creative, and original in the world." The tragedy for her was that "most of us don't fully realize this. Most of us don't realize that when God gave us jazz, he gave the greatest art in the world."[48] Mary Lou's faith emboldened her to have an even richer love for her Black kin.

Mary Lou's faith defied narratives of the angry and tragically self-destructive jazz genius. Her compositions, performances, and recordings were enhanced by her religion, a religion that she found peace through the mysteries of Holy Communion with Christ and His Church. As a Catholic she found a way to reconcile her inner struggles and push outward. Mary Lou's Elijah-like search, her inner history, was demonstrably public. Though she found inner resolution, she never forgot there was an outward struggle with institutional structures that prevented others around her from the fullness of life. This is why she gathered young people around her to teach, to tell them to love themselves, in workshops, churches, and concert halls. Music was entertaining, but it was also a way to go out into the world, make a love offering to "the race."

Mary Lou was an extraordinary American artist, ranking with the best musicians and composers of her era. When she was photographed in Harlem at the famous photo shoot called a "Great Day in Harlem," she was invited there because she was a master pianist. When she became a catechized Catholic she submitted her musical talents to her church, a church that brought her peace with herself and her God. Her gift in return to the Roman Catholic Church was the mystery of the blues, that the long syncopated democratic and revolutionary struggle for freedoms that came in the sounds of dirges and spirituals, field hollers and lining hymns, Blue grass banjoes and rag pianos, rump shaking percussion and whaling trumpets. The Blues was an aesthetic that expressed a range of voices and emotions blurring the sacred and the profane. Mary Lou's aesthetics on piano was born of the Blues, her blues and that of the worlds. It was out of her blues heterodoxy that sprang forth her creative saintliness.

It has been over forty years since I walked in to Schoolkids Records and heard Mary Lou Williams's exquisite artistry in *Praise the Lord* on *Live at the Cookery*. She would live for four more years, until 1981, when she died of bladder cancer at peace with herself in Durham, North Carolina. In the latter half of her life she used her considerable talents for the greater good of serving her fellow musicians who were destitute and inspiring young people to explore their artistry. Her death came at a moment in my life when I was contemplating what theological liberation meant and voraciously reading as many theological liberationists as I could. I had no idea then that her opuses, beginning with the recordings of *Black Christ of the Andes* and *Mary Lou's Mass*, had musically anticipated my own search for a more just and peaceful world.

# 3

# I am free to be what I want to be: Muhammad Ali

In 1964, as Mary Lou's *Black Christ of the Andes* was being released, a convert to Islam was preparing to shake up the world.

The first thing I remember about Muhammad Ali was the mouth. I was seven years old when then-Cassius Clay fought Sonny Liston. It was the first sporting event in my recollection. It was the talk of my New Orleans neighborhood from Dryades down to Washington Ave and back up LaSalle to Simon Bolivar. My uncle and his friends discussed this fight vociferously. They believed that Liston would easily defeat Clay. My uncle and his crew were all born after Jack Johnson. Johnson, the first Black heavyweight-boxing champion, defied cultural standards of being a humble champion. His pride and individuation was globally an *Unforgivable Blackness*.[1] For my uncle's crew there were two kinds of boxing masculinities. The first was Joe Louis, the Brown Bomber; the quiet earnest Alabama-born champion with the big fist. A man lets his fist talk. And there was the streetwise, hip, tight-lipped Sugar Ray Robinson whose hair was perfectly permed and coiffed except when throwing jabs. His manliness was jazz cool—sharp suits and a gorgeous woman on his arm. Sugar Ray was sweet, meaning a worldly man who settled things in the ring or the kind of guy who could take it outside.

What stands out for me was that my uncle's crew, his childhood friends and army buddies, got clean like Sugar Ray. They purchased new suits and shoes to view the fight at a New Orleans movie theater. They were cut, wigged, pressed, cologne and perfumed up. Wives, girlfriends, and mistresses accompanied that crew, as I would discover in later years.

The tickets for the fight were supposed to be sold only in integrated theaters, but there was too much money to be made in all-Black theaters to comply. And all of them wagered on Liston, the Bear, as he was nicknamed. They were stunned when the kid with the mouth won! The defeat of Liston shook up the world. It certainly shook up the small world of my neighborhood.

That boxing match was discussed for weeks afterward, including a religious discussion that I did not understand. Clay, it was said, had become a Muslim. I did not know what a Muslim was then, but I knew it somehow outraged people, even those who did not attend church or were considered irreligious. Whatever it meant for him to be a Muslim was more upsetting than Ali's defeat of Liston. It would take another six years and a move to Chicago for me to have some insight into what being a Muslim meant. By that time, Cassius Marcellus Clay had been fully transformed by faith, name, and anti-Vietnam war dissenter to Muhammad Ali.

I grew up in the pluralism of the Black Christian world. It was Protestant and it was Catholic, sprinkled with tales of Hoodoo and Voodoo. I knew nothing of the formal tenets of Islam. I knew Judaism was different because of the synagogue two blocks from my New Orleans home, but Jews were White. My world in the main was Christian, and it varied only by style, education, and class aspirations. In fact, I understood the assassination of Malcolm X was not because he was a Muslim, but because he had been an outspoken martyr in the cause of Black freedoms. He was like the four little girls bombed in Birmingham—Addie Mae Collins, Carol McNair, Carole Robertson, and Cynthia Wesley—plus murdered Mississippian Medgar Evers. They died in a war waged for civil freedoms that as a kid left me baffled. I am sure there were just as many heated discussions about Malcolm X, but I just don't remember it the way I do regarding Ali's decision to become a "Black Muslim." It was not until we moved to Chicago where the headquarters of the NOI are located that I fully became aware of Black Muslims with an expressive explosion of politics and theology in *Muhammad Speaks, The Black Panther*, and *The Chicago Defender*. I wanted to know how was Ali related to Malcolm, Elijah Muhammad, and the NOI and just what did it mean to be a Black Muslim as opposed to being a Muslim? In the middle of that ring was Ali.

Here's how I learned Ali's story. Minister Malcolm brought him to the faith, but quickly the wizened Elijah Muhammad stole Ali from the morally superior and political progressive minister. With the assassination of Minister Malcolm, the minions of Elijah Muhammad influenced this young impressionable convert and kept him in the NOI. Elijah Muhammad would assign his son, Jabir Herbert, to be at Ali's side and keep guard over his development as he replaced Minister Malcolm as the number one attraction to join the NOI. Most of my information came from Alex Haley's *The Autobiography of Malcolm X*, published after Malcolm's death as he had prophetically predicted. In Haley's telling, X was truly charismatic and religious, not the asthmatic and wheezing messenger. Elijah deceived his followers, but X was authentic. The NOI was not a real religious community without Minister Malcolm; it was a regressive nationalist organization that used religion to disguise its family business. The fuller truth was much more complicated.[2]

Later in college, I began to explore scholarly writings on the NOI. These were published in the early 1960s and they built off the 1959 CBS News documentary narrated by Mike Wallace and Louis Lomax, *The Hate that Hate Produced*. The books were C. Eric Lincoln's *The Black Muslims in America* (1961) and Nigerian scholar E. U. Essien-Udom's *Black Nationalism: A Search for an Identity in America* (1962). These scholars provided sociological frameworks for the religious community. The other book ample in its insight into the NOI was James Baldwin's 1963 *The Fire Next Time*. These books were my source material along with Elijah Muhammad's catechism *Message to a Black Man*. All of these texts offered insight into the NOI as a faith community.

The NOI developed in a spiritual market place, entrepreneurial and efficacious communities of healing and charlatanries. The NOI shared with the Church of God in Christ, the Saints of Christ, the Church of God, the Moorish Science Temple, and Black Jews attempts to build communities not bound by racialist identities. These congregants sought larger ethical and transcendent meaning in a world governed by politically reinforced tautologies that being Black, poor, and dispossessed was an original sin, a sinfulness that required societal punishment.[3]

One's sympathy grows following the biographical details of Elijah (Poole) Muhammad's life. He was born in 1897 in Georgia at the nadir of racial segregation. As husband and wife, Clara and Elijah Muhammad suffered the fate of every Black woman or man of their era. They endured the American South, suffering from the emotional and economic insecurities and dangers that caused them to migrate from Georgia to Detroit in search of "the warmth of other suns."[4] However, the continuous racist humiliations were unrelenting, even in the North where Clara and Elijah ultimately found themselves under the religious tutelage of W. S. Fard. Fard came to Detroit in 1930 and instituted what would eventually become the NOI. His teachings literally lifted Elijah out of the drunkard's gutter, and he and Clara began expounding a faith that they believed offered a greater human destiny for their people. And it ought to be stated there would be no faith organization had it not been for Clara Muhammad. Historian Ula Taylor states it succinctly, "In short, what became the Nation of Islam was driven by a woman."[5] She kept both her household and the NOI organized when Elijah was personally struggling and later imprisoned for evading the draft. She, alongside her husband, kept the dream of a harmonious Black community alive as a faith. The Muhammads worked strenuously to build the community they wish to live in. Their sentiments were a religious mixtape inventively reconfigured the racist world they encountered. Black people were the angels and White people were the fallen angels, devils! This might have seemed crazy from an outsider's perspective, but that was the idea.

Muhammad aimed to turn the world upside down cosmologically. How else to give account for a system of slavery and racial scapegoating that had been continuously heaped on Black America? In his system, there could be no reconciliation or forgiveness where Whites legally and festively condoned lynching. Blacks and Whites were irreconcilable. The faith that the members of the NOI needed had to be as outrageous as America's outlandish brute racial regime.

The NOI was never orthodox in terms of Sunni, the most dominant practice of Islam. Muslim immigrants from the Middle East lived within the bounds of Sunni Islamic practices that were born from the competing pressures and conflicts of Southwest Asian and African histories in the seventh century CE. The fanning out of Islam via the Arab invasion into Rome, collapsing the hold of Rome's colonies in North Africa, helped to shape the formation of an Arab ethnic identity. That identity dominated the ways Islamic history was told. Many Muslim immigrants from Arabic-speaking of regions of Asia and Africa upheld anti-Black mythology based upon the biblical curse of Ham, a narrative that was largely used to reinforce the East African slave trade in the nineteenth century. The Hamitic mythology also found common cause with American southern slaveholders who believed the sons and daughters of Ham were God-ordained to be their slaves.[6] Therefore Middle Eastern Muslim immigrants were not immune from anti-Black bigotry as they attempted to Americanize.

"Islam," Elijah Muhammad told his followers, "was the true religion of the Black man." He wanted to accord his followers an identity that transcended their racial confinement. This was good thing, but Islam, no less than Christianity, had been a religion that supported slaveholding and trading, as well as subjugation—a troublesome, yet relevant fact. It was logical that the NOI was not orthodox. How could it be? The NOI, like the Black Americans experience, was heterodox—it could not fit in, however much Black people tried to squeeze their lives into other people's boxes, religious or otherwise.

Ali "shook up the world" with his defeat of Liston, his victory over a feared opponent afforded him a spiritual certitude about his newfound faith, even as his conversion outrageously offended American sportswriters more. In Thomas Hauser's 1992 *Muhammad Ali: His Life and Times*, many of the sports reporters he interviewed attempted to clean up their reporting. In retrospect, it is evident rereading those reports that racism and class assumptions dripped from them. Reporters who covered Ali with few exceptions had little identification with the twenty-two-year-old's decision to convert to an unorthodox American religious movement. They could not fathom pernicious daily racism that Black persons experienced. These reporters had little sense of their own history let alone the disaffection of Black struggle. And more importantly they had no idea of Ali's inner life.[7] They knew nothing of the communities from which the athletes they reported came or how American history impacted their lives. They couldn't see that Ali's parents, though decent and hardworking, were subjected to the constancy of Louisville's "polite" racism.[8] Kentuckians were politer than Alabamians, but Black folk nevertheless knew their "place," even in the upper South. Journalists who covered Ali and other Black athletes in this period wrote stories as though they were physically powerful minstrels.[9]

The tension over his conversion was not just among journalists; his and his brother's shift in faith also upset Ali's parents. They were Black Baptists and that meant something to them. They had taught their sons to be God-fearing men, moral men. They believed, especially Ali's mother, that she was safeguarding her sons' souls. Immortality was at stake. The NOI was a competitor for the hearts and minds of young people in the religious marketplace. This competition raised all types of fears. Few people leave the faith of their birth. However, Ali and scores of others made this trek from one faith tradition to another. It terrified Black Christian clerics, churches, and their families, even Ali's mother and father. So, this begs the question: What did Ali find in the NOI that he did not find in the Baptist community in which he was reared? Ali's biographer Jonathan Eig has found one of the few things Ali himself copied down about why the NOI was appealing to him. Ali observed:

> The Cartoon was about the first slaves that arrived in America, and the Cartone was showing how Black Slaves were slipping off of the Plantation to pray in Arabic Language facing East. And the White slave Master would Run up Behind the slave ship with a wip and hit the poor little [slave] on the Back with the Wip and say What are you doing praying in the Languid, you what I told you to speak to, and the slave said yes sir yes sir Master, I will pray to Jesus, sir Jesus, and I liked that cartoon it did something to me.[10]

In the NOI he found an answer to the question as to why Black Americans suffered historically. In the NOI's version of Islam he could luxuriate in the goodness and power of his own Blackness.

Ali and X's brotherhood was significant. While other brothers brought Ali in the NOI fold, Malcolm X immediately recognized what the dynamism of Cassius Clay as a religious inquirer would do for the visibility of the religious body. The problem was that the internecine struggles between X and Elijah Muhammad over the future of the NOI tore that brotherhood asunder. X's fatal mistake was not heeding Elijah Muhammad's warning against publicly discussing the assassination of President John F. Kennedy. Unfortunately for X, he bit on the proverbial apple of the New York press. His comments were used against him as being disloyal against the elder Muhammad's divine calling as the leader. This also allowed others, including Elijah Muhammad's sons to organizationally isolate him. It also forced the young adherent to choose between X's faith and desires to make the NOI a stronger political advocate and Elijah Muhammad's cautious quietism. As a faithful, Ali chose to stay in the fold denouncing his brotherhood with X. As a believer, he chose to stay within the community that formed his new Muslim identity. He was driven more by piety than politics. His spiritual transformation was political enough for him at that time.[11]

Ali did not join a militant secular organization like the Revolutionary Action Movement or Student Non-Violent Coordinating Committee or the future Black Panther Party. He expressed his demands for human fairness and decency by joining a religious movement. A religious movement that spoke not to his material needs but his inner self. This is why NOI members who knew him reached out to him. They proselytized him in the same way as his Baptist, Methodist, and Pentecostal counterparts. Being reared a Baptist, Ali knew an altar call; he had been prepped by religious instruction and family orientation to receive a spiritual message.[12] His NOI brothers helped shepherd him into a faith and a community where God created Blackness and it was good.

NOI doctrine positively affirmed Blackness. Though many Christian congregants positively affirmed Blackness too, it was often viewed as muted. Black Christian ethical doctrines regarding humility and long sufferance seemed weak in terms of emancipatory power. And Elijah Muhammad exploited this truth regarding American Christianity. It had been the bedrock of Black oppression. The NOI's dogma was unabashed in proclaiming that Allah was on the side of Black people. Elijah Muhammad's teachings were never meant for White audiences.

It was the reporter Louis Lomax's effort to make a national name for himself that allowed the American White public to discover the NOI. Lomax's journalistic freedom brought the story of the NOI to CBS News, which sensationally produced the television documentary *The Hate that Hate Produced*. In it the American public only saw hatred in this religion that was newly introduced to them.

But the NOI's teachings were a Black theodicy, an explanation as to why Allah permitted evil against Black folk in the world. Why was there Black oppression and what was Allah's plan on behalf of Black people? Allah affirmed the working-class, ex-convicts, and the drug addicted. Their ambitions for the good life could be met in the NOI's religious community. Ali, alongside his sisters and brothers, found this bold heterodoxy life-affirming. Although Ali was driven single-mindedly to be the most dominant boxer of his era, he had an urgent desire to be a part of something greater and seemingly timeless as a young Black man. In the NOI's schema the former Cassius Clay was no minstrel joke or object of scorn or pitied soul, he was a Muslim, a faithful follower of Allah. He had a spiritual destiny. As *Sports Illustrated* magazine reporter Hutson Horn observed, "Ali believed. Nobody entered the Nation of Islam for laughs."[13]

## What's my name?

Ali's conversion and name change was an act of self-narration wonderfully rich as Frederick Bailey who became Frederick Douglass. It was a new story, a self-defined story. This is what it meant for him to accept his new name:

> Changing my name was one of the most important things that happened to me in my life. It freed me from the identity given to my family by slavemasters. . . . People change their names all the time, and no one complains. Actors and actresses change name. The pope changes his name. If I changed my name from Cassius Clay to something like Smith or Jones because I wanted a name that white people thought was more American, nobody would have complained. I was honored that Elijah Muhammad gave me a truly beautiful name. "Muhammad" means one worthy of praise. "Ali" was the name of a great general [a cousin of the Prophet Muhammad, and the third Caliph after the death of the Prophet].[14]

From a boxing ring no one anticipated that his name change would start a contentious rile and a religious battle within Black America. Boxing, like any other sport, has never been about one's affiliation. Though athletes make religious gesticulations as signs of their faith and communal identities, it in the end has little bearing on the outcome. Sports is about the mastery of particular bodily skills, physical strength, and strategies that will lead one to win over one's opponent or team. Yet, in the first championship match, Muhammad Ali versus Floyd Patterson, it would play itself out as America's version of the Crusades. Here was the irony: these opponents shared the sufferings of being Black in America, but they unwittingly brought Muslim and Christian histories into the center ring.

Ali's boxing championship, like Jack Johnson's before, made him an enemy of the state. The search for "a Great White Hope" to defeat Johnson had ballooned into a global racial panic. Johnson's bravado was a stark reminder to Anglo-Europeans as to why "the darker races," needed to be pacified. Johnson's challengers represented in the collective imagination of Anglo-Europeans the global superiority of White virility.

After Johnson, by the mid-twentieth century, Black athletes were important to the general society in terms of their representation of the larger geopolitical interests of the state—Joe Louis against Italy's Primo Carnera and Germany's Max Schmeling, and Jesse Owens's triumphant medals sweep at the 1936 Olympics in Berlin are just two examples. Even the American baseball player, Jackie Robinson, seemed to symbolically represent in the post–Second World War era the United States as a racially inclusive democracy. The reality of American apartheid, of course, was quite different, but American interests were paramount, even if those interests had to be advanced sometimes by Black bodies.

Ali as a Black Muslim did not accept the secular theology of American dream and its supporting religious linkages. Floyd Patterson was a man who struggled to refashion himself, a man whose narrative was one that any member of the NOI including Malcolm X could have appreciated—Southern migration, impoverishment, reform school, a Roman Catholic conversion, and boxing as a way out economically. Had Patterson been bigger and faster he might have owned Ali's legacy as a champion heavyweight boxer. Instead, Patterson believed his opponent's conversion was an affront to the type of orthodoxy he had striven to build for himself. Patterson had framed himself as being socially acceptable well before he encountered Ali.

Patterson and Ali had competing ideas about what it meant to be respected. Patterson believed that Black people could and should be a part of the American establishment as insiders. His conversion as a Roman Catholic gave him clear moral teachings, spiritual fortitude, and legitimacy and status within an important American institution.[15] Like Mary Lou Williams, Patterson converted to Catholicism following the Second World War just as the church attempted to bury its virulent anti-Semitism born of the inquisition. This virulence was exemplified by Detroit's Father Joseph Coughlin, a venomous anti-Semite whose national radio broadcast from the Church of the Little Flower was barely mentioned by the American church's hierarchy by the late 1940s. When Patterson joined the Roman Catholic Church its public appeal across the United States was being Americanized by the likes of the genial televised bishop, Fulton Sheen, whose earlier anti-communist homilies turned toward more general appeals of Catholic moral goodness in the 1960s. Patterson had no sense of recent Catholic history. Patterson wanted to be accepted as an American. He did not want to be seen as socially deviant outside the American mainstream. His Catholicism he believed made him acceptable.

In 1962, Patterson teamed with Milton Gross to cowrite the boxer's autobiography *Victory Over Myself*. Patterson found this relationship pleasing. He teamed with Gross once again to write a story for *Sports Illustrated* titled "I Want to Destroy Clay." Patterson argued that the boxing championship was global and that whoever was champion had to represent virtues. He noted that he had been warned by former UN representative not to engage Sonny Liston because of his prior criminal convictions. He dismissed this because he believed that holding the championship title brought out the best in people who had not been given a fair chance in life. Liston had to be given a chance. However, Ali was different. According to Patterson he had "practically turned over the title to the Black Muslims."[16] He shifted tone. He was no longer discussing the virtues of being a champion boxer and how that would aid Black communities toward equal citizenship. Nor was he saying like Michael Jordan once offered in competitive rage that he wanted to completely destroy the Detroit Pistons basketball team. Patterson made it personal about Ali's religious faith. "Because of that I cannot respect him as a champion or as a man," he penned. He viewed Ali's self-transformation as a NOI member as being deleterious to the cause of both Civil Rights and Black people generally.

Just in case we forget Patterson saw his own Roman Catholic conversion as universalizing him and giving him more self-respect and respect for all human beings. He framed his self around promulgation of church doctrine that insisted that baptism made all one in Christ. He recognized the notion of "universal love" did not always extend to include Black Americans in the church to which he pledged his allegiance. Nevertheless, this was his guiding faith. Patterson, however, assessed the NOI as being a hate group. "They preach hate and separation instead of love. They preach mistrust when there must be understanding," he continued. "Clay is so young and has been misled by the wrong people that he doesn't appreciate how far we have come and how much harm he has done by joining the Black Muslims. He might have well joined the Ku Klux Klan." Patterson's assessment was that "one undemocratic organization is as bad as another. Put these two groups together on a desert island and after a while you wouldn't be able to tell a Black Muslim from a white bed sheet."[17] Of course, there were distinctions to be made. The NOI never told its membership to launch a wholesale attack on anyone because they were White. And there were more ironies to Patterson's claims. The NOI by all measures was a conservative religious group. It called on its members to be family oriented with men leading the family. It promoted small businesses and healthy living dietary-wise. Ironically, all the personal behavioral ethics that Patterson found in the Roman Catholic Church were the same as the NOI. The difference was that the NOI put Black self-regard as central to its theology as a religious organization. In the heat of the moment Patterson could not see the commonalities that his faith tradition had with his opponent. His commentary made a boxing bout a Black-inflected Crusade—noble Christians against Black undesirable Muslims. Religiously and culturally, it was a stunning statement by Patterson.

Ali would retort calling Patterson an Uncle Tom. Now, I am sure Harriet Beecher Stowe had no idea when she wrote her 1852 anti-slave novel that her depiction of a superbly virtuous enslaved man, based on the realities of Josiah Henson who endured slavery's brutality, would become a ferocious accusation of being the worse type of sellout.[18] As historian William Jeremiah Moses explains, Uncle Tom the character never started out to be a pejorative. The most outspoken Black nationalists considered the character virtues that Stowe fictionally described in Tom—patience, humility, altruism, and kindness—as virtues. These ethical characteristics were about building up a mighty race.[19] However, by the time it came out of Ali's mouth it was poisonous. Uncle Tom was a quisling, a traitor to his people. Minister Malcolm X had publicly used the trope of Uncle Tom often. He too neatly pigeonholed what it was like to be a slave by dichotomizing it into house versus field slaves. House slaves were easily categorized by the claim that they easily identified with the system that brutally subjugated those held in bondage. It was historically an inaccuracy, but it stuck. X's ideas were really about class divides in Black communities. The young Ali was a rebellious Nat Turner with a Quran instead of a Bible.

What was played out in the ring between these two men's faiths was long held notions regarding masculinity and manhood. Christianity in its earliest history was seen as an effeminate religion. Jesus was not much of a god-like man if the Roman could execute him. Notions of the cause of God's love did not make much sense in the Roman world. A god had to demonstrate power. This religion was a faith for women, not for men. This line of reasoning continued until the fourth century CE when Constantine the Byzantine emperor made his peace with Christianity and it became the religion of the Byzantine state. As a state religion Christianity would have to align itself with the martial elements of the state. Its spiritual emphasis on a political community governed by love, the Kingdom of God, would have to be whittled away so that bloody warlords and ravaging explorers could be faithful Christians too. Jesus's radical notion of a peaceable kingdom in the Constantine era came under control by a hierarchy of male priests with the Bishop of Rome becoming the dominant bishopric. They would dictate what the true faith would look like. Christianity, having escaped the peaceable spiritual emphasis of some its earliest women communicants, became a faith run by men, but lived by women.

Throughout the gospel writings, especially Luke's recounting of the earliest formation of Christianity as it separated from its Judaism and the Pauline epistles, women were everywhere as important laborers and evangelists in building Christianity as a religious movement. However, by the fourth century, a male hierarchy led by bishops who feudally called themselves "Princes of the Church" controlled the movement. The religion became martial faith used to justify conquest in the name of spreading the Gospel of Christ.

Islam was equally martial in its rendering from the Caliphates and the Arabic invasion across North Africa as it defeated the former colonies of the collapsing Roman Empire. By the seventh century, when the Prophet Muhammad returned from Medina to Mecca, prayer was linked to conquering other lands in the name of Allah. Similarly, like Christianity, Islam established hierarchal male Caliphates and a male clerical system led by Imams. They controlled the official theology and Arabic, the sacred and holy language of the Muslim. Islam would have its internal conflicts too, found in its varying schools of law. Shi'a versus Sunni and the spiritualism of Sufism made for lively debates in every Muslim region. Like its Christian and Jewish counterparts there would be debates about what the Prophet Muhammad meant. For instance, was jihad primarily a declared war, a *Fatwa*, to overthrow non-Muslims infidels, especially those religions that did not conform to the Quran like the Torah or Christian New Testament? Or did jihad mean something different, the warring of one's conscience and spirit—like in the Pauline sense of the warring within the self to be righteous?

Islam and Christianity as religious ideologies framed political modernity beginning with the unification of Spain under Catholicism in the fifteenth century and the rise of the Islamic Ottoman Empire. This competition lasted between the "West" and the Ottoman Empire until the latter began a slow erosion in the eighteenth century. That erosion was framed in terms of male muscularity; the collapsing Ottoman Empire was referred to as "the sick man of Europe."

The Protestant revolution redrew the maps of Europe. It turned the continent's political governance from polylingual kingdoms toward monolingual nation-states. In other words, language and governance became synonymous with one another; one's ethnicity and government aligned. The United States was a new type of country—ruled by Anglo-Protestants who were distrustful of the old countries in Europe with their anti-Christian popery. And they were equally distrustful of those far off Mohammadans, as the archaic English termed "Muslims," who supported "white slavers" and pirates. The US Marine Corp hymn has left us enough cultural evidence as to the way this distrustful history is remembered—"From the Halls of Montezuma/To the shores of Tripoli . . ."

Of course, these Mohammadans varied from region to region. They were West Africans in what were obscure places in the American imagination—Senegal, Guinea, and Nigeria. There the jihads episodically began in Guinea's highland, the Futa Jallon, led by the Fulani to end corruption in theory and bring about theocratic states. These struggles became strongholds against British and French imperialism. These Muslims resisters would come to loom large in the imagination of 1960s Black nationalists. They would ignore that there were a variety of resisters to the European and British encroachment, as well as to the institution of slavery. Nationalists would not bother to think carefully about Muslims' traffic in slaves or centralized states throughout West Africa. However, these anti-imperialist resisters would be looked upon heroically and they played into the Honorable Elijah Muhammad's notion that Islam was "the natural religion of the Black man."

As for Floyd Patterson, being Roman Catholic was superior to Black Protestantism, with its links to slavery, wide-open spiritual marketplace, entrepreneurial preachers, and highly democratic and eclectic church polity. Being a Catholic for Patterson gave him social status in the 1950s. The Roman Catholic Church after the Second World War had arrived; it was now an American church. It was acceptable publicly to be Catholic, the faith had become, in a sense, whitened. Ethnic ties with provincial nations such as Ireland, Poland, Czechoslovakia, and Italy were dissipating and Catholics were entering the major elite universities attaining Kennedyesque respectability. As a Black Catholic, Patterson felt he deserved the same type of welcome Eastern Europeans and Italians had recently earned.

From the instruction of the Honorable Elijah Muhammad, Ali learned an independent spirituality. It did not matter that a White-run religious hierarchy conferred acknowledgment upon Black people. Black humanity was above being defined by an oppressive European institution. After all, the Roman Catholic Church's lengthy institutional history was stained with the blood of millions through the transatlantic slave trade. Papal Bulls condoned the business of slavery and they set up chapels in the fortresses of the slave trade, praying for the souls of European mercenaries. The Catholic Church's teachings had pacified the minds of Black people in the same way that Black Protestantism mollified Black people's will to resist racist oppression. In Patterson and Ali, two men who shared many commonalities were fighting a religious history they were not fully of aware in the name of Black liberation.

One believed that the Catholic Church gave him the spiritual reinforcement to be seen as acceptable in American society; the other believed in a spirituality that warded off the vile forces that American society had historically spewed on its Black citizens. Each man desired the best for their community; each of them wanted recognition, as well as opportunity for the people they believed they represented.

The actual boxing match between the two men was not much. Ali dominated the bout from start to finish. Athletically, Ali was the superior boxer. He toyed with Patterson, refusing to knock him out over the twelve rounds. It was humiliating and frustrating for Patterson. Ali had made his points. He was the greater boxer and his faith and membership in the NOI was not lesser than Patterson's Roman Catholicism. But although Ali proved he was the greater boxer, the bout did not prove whose notion of God or whose faith was more liberating for Black people. Liberation, politically, personally or religiously, always depends on context and circumstances. Outside the ring, however, a critical minority among Black Americans was challenging the antidemocratic forces historically embedded in American legality and culture that were allied against their human rights.

Floyd Patterson athletically was no challenge to Ali, who defended his title and his faith easily by humiliating and punishing him in the ring. Two years later, in 1967, Ali would be crueler to his opponent Ernie Terrell. By Terrell's account he and Ali shared a boxing camaraderie if not a shallow friendship. Early on in their relationship, in 1962, Terrell recollected Ali's infatuation with the NOI and how Ali had stopped at a historically Black College in Tennessee attempting to witness to his faith. According to Terrell:

He was popular because he was an Olympic champion, but nothing like what came later. And he tried to talk to some of the students. There was a group of ten or twelve of them, and he was talking about black people

being stripped of their identity in the United States: except back then, most
people used the word "Negro." And the students were relating to what he
said. Times were different. He was saying, "If you see a Chinaman, you
know he comes from China. If you see a Canadian, you know he comes
from Canada. If you see a Frenchman, you know comes from France."
Then he asked, "Now tell me, what country is called 'Negro'?" And one of
the students looked at him and said, 'I don't know, but I never heard of a
country called "white folk" either.'[20]

The student's dismissive attitude angered Ali. Terrell's recollection is important
because it offers insight into Ali's hope to convert his peers to the NOI. The
young Ali was fully convinced of the rightness of his position. In *Black Muslim
Religion in the Nation of Islam, 1960-1975* the scholar of American Islam,
Edward Curtis IV, offers an important distillation as to how the NOI attempted
to reshape the consciousness of its members. The NOI was a Muslim movement
that attempted to address the needs of persons who had been shaped as Black
Protestants. The aspirations of Black Americans could find fulfillment inside
the NOI's religious community. With this new faith came a new sense of self
and self-explanation. The honorable Elijah Muhammad had gleaned well from
his study of the Bible and the Pauline epistles that self-transformation required
new clothes. Here was Black radicalism not in secular anti-theistic rhetoric,
but through complete religious transformation.

According to Terrell, he never meant any disrespect by calling Ali by his
birth name. However, one might wish to take that with a grain of salt. Terrell
was using the name Cassius Clay to get into Ali's psyche to distract him in
preparation for the fight. That strategy proved to be a mistake.

Ali was an angry man. In his mind, Terrell's disrespect was the icing on
the cake. He had put up with two years of press affronts about his faith, but
he would not put up with from a fellow boxer he shared so much with. And
while Terrell's religious biography is murky, the era and region in which he

was born and the place he was born is suggestive. Terrell was born in 1939 in Belzoni, Mississippi, in the Delta region that cut across Arkansas, Tennessee, Mississippi, Louisiana, and Alabama. Religion was in full bloom as was cotton. It was the homes of Baptists, Holiness folk, and Pentecostals, and out of these spaces came the latter half of twentieth-century music—the Blues and the Gospel Blues and the likes of Reverend C. L. Franklin and B. B. King. As a Black Southerner Terrell shared with Ali a rearing and moral guidance in the spirited and eclectic world of Black Protestant culture. Each man had attended Sunday school and sung the communal hymnody of their churches. This instruction taught them on how to behave publicly, if not privately. The two boxers shared a religious and moral indoctrination. The irony of their moral foundation was it set the ground of Ali's conversion and Terrell's insensitivity to it.

By every report Ali humiliated Terrell more than he did Patterson. He taunted him with punishing jabs as he shouted, "What's my name? Nigger, what's my name?" This fight was about respect. Ali treated Terrell cruelly. He held Terrell in a headlock and dragged his cut eye along the ropes. It was perhaps something he wanted to do to White reporters who repeatedly taunted in him writing with a thousand slights against his faith. Terrell looked back on the bout as though he did not mean to offend the champion. However, given time and hindsight, his claim cannot fully be believed. There was a fierce competition between Black Protestants and the NOI. Black urban preachers feared the encroachment of the NOI worse than they did the competition with one another for parishioners. The NOI was perceived as threat to the primacy of Black churches. The members that the NOI sought, especially men, were those left behind in the upward mobility of Black congregants.

Ali, after the assassination of Malcolm X, was unofficially the public spokesperson for the NOI; he was an evangelist, a defender of the faith. In the competition between the NOI and Black Protestant institutions he was teaching Black people a lesson even in the ring. His faith was not subservient to forms of Christian humility. Submission to Allah meant that as a male it was his God-given right to have respect; Black Muslims represented self-respecting manhood. The Christian virtues of "Uncle Tom" whose fate was constrained by institutional circumstances were now no longer acceptable to Black people in the face of continuing segregation, racism, and harsh treatment. Being a Black Muslim allowed one to call out the blunt brutality of White folk's religion and their cruel dominance over Black people publicly. Theologically for Ali, Uncle Tom's humble faith was self-inflicted slavery. White sports reporters did not have the right to script him or his faith, nor did an unaware Black boxer who unwittingly cooperated with an ideology of White dominance. Brutally defeating Terrell everyone now knew he was no "Uncle Tom," and that his name was Muhammad Ali, a Black Muslim, a fighting one and a loyal member of the NOI.

## Enemy of the state

Ali's conversion made him an enemy of the state. When he joined the NOI he was persona non-grata. The Federal Bureau of Investigation (FBI) had spied on the NOI and Elijah Muhammad for decades prior to Ali becoming a member. As a high-profile athlete Ali's faith choice was taken apoplectically. If Martin Luther King, Jr. disturbed the state as Baptist preacher, Ali's linkages to Elijah Muhammad and Malcolm X were unnerving to the security regime. And the sports writers made sure he was portrayed not just as a Muslim and a boxer, but a person who threatened all that was good about the United States.

Religious faiths have always been a threat to state doctrines from monarchy to nationalisms. History is full of stories of states guarding against religious and spiritual movements. Contemporary history is full of instances—Stalinist Soviet Union's leeriness of the Orthodox Church and deathly fear of Protestant evangelicals or the Chinese government's brutal overreaction to the Falun

Gong or the US government overwrought reactions to radical Islam. The Islamic organization that Elijah Muhammad led was viewed as subversive to American values. Ali's links to the religious community was a subversion that warranted punishment.

Black male athletes who drew national attention before Ali's era—Jesse Owens, Joe Louis, and Jackie Robinson—were made into media symbols of state interests. Ali's faith rejected America's civil mythology. The NOI was outside the bounds of the acceptable religions. As a religious convert, Ali was painted as a naive young man who joined an inauthentic radical sect. His experience anticipated the experiences of Muslims in the United States after 9/11. But Ali was not naive. He joined the NOI sincerely believing in the teaching of the Messenger. In joining the NOI he sacrificed a loving female companion, as well as comfort. He truly wanted to be a faithful Muslim.

Few reporters who wrote about Ali at the time of his conversion understood that his outspokenness on the US military intervention into Vietnam's civil war was in keeping with his faith tradition. Before the Cold War, Black American elites as diverse as W. E. B. DuBois to Elijah Muhammad had admired the rise of Japan in a geopolitical world dominated by Anglo-European nation-states. In the struggle to transform America from a White-denominated democracy to an inclusive democracy, diverse Black voices found inspiration from political mobilization by the "darker peoples" globally. And these mobilizations all had a religious component. For Elijah and Clara Muhammad, W. D. Fard's teachings rang true precisely because they challenged prevailing Christian and political orthodoxies. The call to Mecca was a call to "Asiatic" Blackness, not American Negro-ness. It was a global sacred history. Malcolm X's calls for a domestic like "Bandung Conference," a global anticolonial struggle, in the "Third World" of Harlem in 1950s was built upon the NOI's global sacred history beginning with Fard and carried out by Elijah Muhammad. Muhammad would serve time in federal prison for evading the draft and was under surveillance for tenuous linkages to the Japanese.[21] Muhammad Ali's religious resistance to the draft was fueled by a heterodox history. In 1967, amid his difficulties regarding his refusal of the draft, National Basketball hall of fame player Bill Russell understood and witnessed Ali's faith close-up. He wrote that Ali's conscience was driven by a faith that gave him a strength that was enviable.[22] Though Ali would never claim to be an intellectual, his viewpoints were guided by an alternative history and faith that informed his decision making.

Ali's stance to the draft was initially practical. He was an athlete at the prime of his earning powers. Additionally, he tested poorly, which kept his scores from meeting the minimum military standard. However, the sports press goaded him. They compared him to other Black athletes who had acquiesced, or perhaps chosen to serve out of a sense of patriotic responsibility. Their hounding compelled him to make a statement. His religious conscience shaped by an alternative history regarding Black greatness fostered his religious dissension. "Man," Ali uttered in exasperation, "I ain't got no quarrel with them Vietcong." It was the "gotcha" moment for sports writers like Robert Lipsyte.[23] The press was never concerned about what athletes thought of American foreign affairs except in this instance. Black athletes were silent symbols representative of American exceptionalism, never critics. However, Ali had seen Jackie Robinson's feats of courage off the baseball field, he knew of Jack Johnson's prowess and social defiance, and he was old enough to see Jim Brown up close and personal. These particular athletes seemed to defy fear. The difference between Ali and them was they were not members of a religious organization that was militantly pro-Black.

In the minds of the sportswriters and the public, Ali had to be punished. He had been disloyal to the country simply by virtue of his membership in the NOI. How dare a Black American associate with a religious organization that equated White people with the devil!

Had any of the reporters bothered to read the Bible closely? If they had they might have recognized that religion and religious folk had enemies. Philistines,

Samaritans, Egyptians Babylonians, beastly Romans—all were at one time the enemies of God. Religions often incorporated and sacralized the concept of the "other" as not only different, but evil. This is what has made religious identity so powerful and dangerous historically. The apt example could be the American Ku Klux Klan, as Kelly J. Baker has brilliantly demonstrated in her scholarship on the organization's eclectic Protestantism. However, the press and the politicians punished Ali for his religious affiliation. The NOI as a localized American brand of Islam argued in its cosmology that whiteness was demonic. The Klan believed in sacralized whiteness and used actual terrorism to reinforce its notion of a White-controlled democracy. The NOI had never advocated or gone out to harm Whites, while the Klan had murdered Blacks with impunity. The NOI had advocated self-defense against attack, but never wholesale subjugation of Whites through brutality. However, in the eyes of the state, the NOI was far more subversive than the Klu Klux Klan. False arguments of equivalence were made all the time about the two religious organizations, but the realities were otherwise.

When Ali's case reached the United States Supreme Court, the justices ruled in his favor based on procedural technicalities rather than his religious freedom. The Court was perplexed by a religious organization that viewed White people demonically. It did not know how to the treat the NOI as a religious organization. So, the judges avoided the religious dimensions of Ali's case all together. The Court had established a liberal consensus on the unification of the United States after the Second World War. In their rulings, the justices attempted to hasten the country toward a more inclusive democracy and away from White racialized democracy. The lessons of Nazi Germany loomed large in the era of Civil Rights protest. The court had ruled affirmatively on *Brown v. Board of Education* (1954) to *Loving v. Virginia* (1967), but they did not know what to do with a conscientious objector that did not believe in its liberal consensus on race. The NOI was critical of racial liberalism as defined by the court. They did not believe that Black Americans were beneficiaries of state's liberal largesse; instead, they believed that liberalism, as defined by the court, victimized Black America.

Many admired Ali's resistance to the draft and the Vietnam War. That adoration and support from friends and simpaticos helped him to endure the court battles, state harassment, and public anger. His stance and his ever-ready camera persona helped strengthen other leaders to take a stance against the war too. The Vietnam War was not Black America's fight, though a disproportionate number of Black male soldiers compared to their non-Black military colleagues died in that war. Ali's decision to resist the war in Vietnam, a war that was a gross political error that stemmed from hubris, came at crucial crossroads in US history. Slowly the entire country realized how poorly its national leaders had served them by engaging in it. His victory in the Supreme Court reinforced his faith in Black American righteousness. Allah was on his side and his people's side.

## "This first step is the control and the protection of our own women"

The term "Family values" is an overused term. However, various religious communities and theologies all support marriage and family life as signs of godly order. Religious obeisance, daily disciplines of prayer, alms giving, and fasting are intended to take one from self-centeredness toward consideration for others, especially one's family. Before the term found its way onto the GOP political platform in 1976, as Gerald Ford attempted to counter Jim Carter his Democratic challenger's White Southern Evangelical ties by enshrining the American family as foundational to Republican civil religion. This appealed to Black Christian clergy and Muslim imams. They preached the life of the family was patriarchally ordered by God.[24] Looking at Ali as a Muslim begs the question of his relationship to his wives and family. Taking care of one's family was a tangible sign of faith. In Islam being a good husband, father, and ostensibly the head of the household as a provider is paramount (as it is or has been in Christianity and Judaism). So it is important to examine

Ali as a family man and his relationship to women generally and his wives in particular.[25]

In his catechism, *Message to a Blackman*, Elijah Muhammad outlined the following six points:

1   Allah, Himself, has said that we cannot return to our land until we have a thorough knowledge of our own selves. This first step is the control and the protection of our own women. There is no nation on earth that has less respect for and little control of their women as we so-called Negroes here in America. Even animals and beasts, the fowls of the air, have more love and respect for their females than have the so-called Negroes of America.

2   Our women are allowed to walk or ride the streets all night long, with any strange men they desire. They are allowed to frequent any tavern or dance hall that they like, whenever they like. They are allowed to fill our homes with children other than our own. Children that are often fathered by the very devil himself. Then, when the devil man decides to marry her, the so-called Negro press and magazines will make it front page news. The daily press will not print a so-called Negro man marrying into their race, but you seem to think it is an honor to your own nation when your daughter goes over to your enemies, the devils.

3   Our women have been and are still being used by the devil White race, ever since we were first brought here to these States as slaves. They cannot go without being winked at, whistled at, yelled at, slapped, patted, kicked and driven around in the streets by your devil enemies right under your nose. Yet you do nothing about it, nor do you even protest.

4   You cannot control or protect your women as long as you are in the white man's false religion called Christianity. This religion of theirs gives you no desire or power to resist them. The only way and place to solve this problem is in the Religion of Islam.

5   It is a pleasure to Allah to defend us from our enemies. In the religion of Christianity, the white race has had us worshiping and praying to something that actually did not even exist.

6   Islam will not only elevate your women but will also give you the power to control and protect them. We protect ours against all their enemies.[26]

Women were at the core of the NOI's religious nationalism as historian Ula Taylor has demonstrated.[27] The nearly three centuries-old institution of chattel slavery, the honorable Elijah Muhammad preached, had left the once glorious Black family in tatters. Black women, he believed, were unprotected and subject to rapes by the sexually predacious. Eventually, by the time Black families began leaving the South like his family left Georgia for Detroit, the relationship between Black men and women were destabilized because of low-esteem, White dominance, and a labor market which systematically excluded most Black men. His preachments about the relationship between Black women and men were not much different than his Christian counterparts found in the teachings of the Church of God in Christ, which grew out of the same soil as the NOI.[28] The irony cannot be lost here. The NOI male leaders and followers like Ali were participating in orthodoxies about women's roles, even though they were proclaiming Black communal self-regard. Both the women and men attempted to conform to this orthodoxy even though it was not completely satisfactory in their daily intimacies and interactions. This orthodoxy had sacred approval in both the Bible and the Quran, but the trouble was if one were to read these texts uncritically, the creation narrative of male dominance trapped both women and men in a cruel game of dominance and subordination, not mutuality. Nevertheless, Ali saw the relationship between men and women as foundational to Black community.

Theologically the NOI found contemporary support in the scholarship of sociologist E. Franklin Frazier who penned in 1939 *The Negro Family in the United States.* Frazier depicted the Black family as fractured. It was true and equally true for American families in general. The economic devastation wrought on Black families from years of exploited agricultural toil and the Great Depression had greatly harmed Black families. They were locked out in the South by racist political violence to keep agrarian exploitation intact. The run away from "Feudal America" to the industrial corridors of America had not benefited Black Americans as much as they had dreamed. In Frazier's scheme, the Black family was out of kilter, though surely the economic tide of the Great Depression and shifting attitudes among all Black migrants as they escaped rurality reflected their own changing ideological thinking about family and relationships.[29]

Frazier and Muhammad would differ on the specifics of American Black assimilation, but they agreed that the health of the American Black family was dire. An important principle preached by Elijah Muhammad was that Black families lived under the daily torment of racism and therefore were in need of re-ordering. Black families required strong males as the head of households. The irony of this is that Elijah Muhammad had not always been a personally strong person. Clara, his wife, had kept their family intact for a better part of their years together when he fell adrift. This would also be true of Malcolm X; the ideals of family were one thing but their lived realities were another.[30] Black men and women always had a rough equality coming out of slavery. Religious doctrine and the law held otherwise; they attempted to reinforce female subservience. The doctrine that Elijah Muhammad preached, as did his other religious counterparts, was that God made men the heads of their households. This was the salve to heal the social ills plaguing Black people as a nation. The NOI took special pride on spiritually reshaping dysfunctional Black urban households into self-respecting family units.

The young Muhammad Ali attempted to live his life as faithfully as he possible could. As a man, familial respectability was essential, as taught by Muhammad. The first line in the fight for self-respect was the family and the man of the family was its theoretical head. This indoctrination left an intellectually wide-open lane to justify his sexual behavior outside of his marriage. In other words, as a man he was entitled to do what he pleased. The preachments he heard about the protection of women and male headship opened a door for a confused young man to blow it in relationships with the women he married. My read of Ali from his various biographers is that he tried to live up to the standards of respectability as promoted by his faith, but failed many times until he reached middle age. Fame, handsomeness, and physical prowess at a young age kept him in a quandary. Nothing he learned in his Baptist rearing or his conversion to Islam taught him to think about his sexual desires. Attraction, desire, and emotional commitment in a spousal relationship appeared to be an afterthought in his theological formation as a Muslim and as a former Christian. What is so interesting is that being a boxer was as much about the sexualized body as being a supermodel. Yet the fact was both as a professional boxer and a member of the NOI he held on to antiquated notions about kinship and intimacy. Ali lived in a male echo chamber.

Sonsyrea Tate's compelling memoir *Little X* offers a glimpse into the NOI for a girl coming of age.[31] The religious nationalism may have built pride, but it also constricted the role of women. When Ali joined the NOI, he was equally confused about the meaning of relationships. This should not come as anything unusual or salacious—young men, whether Christian, Jew, or Muslim, are often confused about sexuality and the ethics of sexual relationships. There exist many historical accounts of religious figures struggling with the flesh. So, Ali did not fully work out everything until his last marriage. This did not mean he was not a good father or a loving father; he really attempted to be better than his own father. Nevertheless, he was conflicted, which led him to be disenchanted with his wives and a sense of shame about his own sexual contradictions. Inside the Muslim community women like Tate would rightly point out those contradictions and the emotional neglect women endured. If Ali helped to shape American Blackness in his legendary bouts in the early to mid-1970s, Black women, religious and nonreligious, were coming into a greater articulation of Black women's power. Those articulations only once held in parlors, quilting bees, clubs, and prayer meetings burst into prose and poetry everywhere. Their resistances to male sacralized authority troubled Black men including Ali. Normative ethics justifying manliness through god-talk had finally produced a pushback. Black women asked forcefully what equality before Allah or God meant to Muslim and Christian men alike. Ali faced these tensions from his wives and his daughters.

## I am free to be what I want to be

For Ali, joining the NOI was initially very much about a God who spoke to and redefined the needs of Black people—Black power, Black self-regard, and Black dignity. However, when Elijah Muhammad died in 1975, Ali left the NOI on in his faith. After Muhammad's death, many NOI members moved back to being Christians, but Ali remained a Muslim. He continued to grow in his faith as he followed Imam Warith Deen Mohammed (formerly Wallace D. Muhammad), Elijah and Clara Muhammad's seventh son. Imam Mohammed would found the American Society of Muslims, creating a more universalist sect of Sunni Islam. Minister Louis Farrakhan would continue the legacy of Elijah Muhammad, continuing to address the specific needs of Black Americans, especially the Black working-class and poor, and to keep the NOI going. In this believers' schism between the NOI and the American Society of Muslims, Ali never lost his love for Black Americans, a people for whom he repeatedly stood up even while recognizing the commonality of faith among all ethnicities across the globe.

In 1964, when the young Ali declared his freedom in angry frustration to *New York Times* reporter Robert Lipsyte, he was in a sense declaring it for Black Americans. Lipsyte asked Ali about his decision to join the NOI. Ali remarked that the NOI was deeply moral and he further asserted, "I know where I'm going and I know the truth and I don't have to be what you want me to be. I'm free to be what I want to be." This exchange between Lipsyte and Ali regarding his religious beliefs and his own right of self-determination reflected the experiences of many Black Americans. This is why he intrigued so many in Black communities. For Lipsyte, Ali's comments made for good headlines, for Ali was expressing an opacity regarding his freedom and determining truth for himself. He was in a sense making claims to self-autonomy, the same self-autonomy that the philosopher Kwame Anthony Appiah waxes eloquently about in his masterful *The Ethics of Identity*. Appiah eloquently writes:

> To create a life, in other words, is to interpret the materials that history has given you. Your character, your circumstances, your psychological constitution, including the beliefs and preferences generated by the interaction of your innate endowments and your experience: all these needs to be taken into account in shaping a life. They are not constraints on that shaping; they are its materials. As we come to maturity, the identities we make our individualities, are interpretive responses to our talents and disabilities, and the changing social, semantic, and material contexts we enter at birth; and we develop our identities dialectically with our capacities and circumstances, because the latter are in part the product of what our identities lead us to do. A person's shaping of her life flows from her beliefs and from a set of values, tastes, and dispositions of sensibility, all of these influenced by various forms of social identity: let us call these together a person's ethical self.[32]

Appiah's argument regarding notions of self-autonomy centers upon the utilitarian reasoning of the philosopher John Stuart Mill whereas Ali's self-autonomy used the teachings of Elijah Muhammad. He assented to belonging to a community of believers that brought him meaning and understanding as a young Black American living in a society defined by the racist logic of empire.

In the years after his legendary boxing career, Ali became more accommodating to state power. Like Eldridge Cleaver, Justice Clarence Thomas, and others, he would try to shoehorn a Black self-help tradition into an American political conservatism. In this effort, he would endorse Ronald Reagan for president—Reagan, whose stridency against the politics of the Black Panther Party worked to help destroy the California base organization. In this decision Ali made a pragmatic choice in an effort to secure his family's financial well-being. He and his family would have to be seen as nonthreatening to American political elite in order to thrive. Second, Reagan's speechmaking in theory fit squarely with aspects of religious nationalism that Ali had ingested in his decision to join the NOI. As a result of his strategic endorsement of Reagan, the political and corporate leaders helped turn him into an American global ambassador just as the governing institutions in the Middle East collapsed, the Cold War receded, and a new struggle ensued with the United States beginning with the Iranian hostage crisis. The militarized secular old regimes squared off with young radicals who dreamed of a utopic Islam in the age of the Caliphates.

Paradoxically, Ali, who youthfully criticized the likes of Joe Louis for his symbolic representation of the American imperial power during the Second World War, functioned as retired boxer in a similar symbolic role as Louis. He was the United States's Muslim ambassador. In 1996, witnessing Ali's run with the Olympic torch in Atlanta was a poignant globally televised moment. The image of Ali, suffering severely from Parkinson's disease, walking swiftly and determinedly with the Olympic torch and lighting the Olympic flame in the hometown of Dr. Martin Luther King, Jr. will be indelibly remembered. He had come full circle from the apocryphal accounts that he threw his gold medal he won in the 1960 Olympics in the river because of his discontentment with his country. In Atlanta, he represented American exceptionalism, the sense that the democracy in the United States was big enough to accept and make space for a once-brash young Black American who boldly declared his freedom and joined a radical indigenous American Islam. Wittingly or unwittingly, he had become every bit as symbolic as Joe Louis.

Ali's faith story, with all his political and personal inconsistencies, touched the lives of many as he exemplified self-expression and freedom of conscience. Even at the height of his Muslim conversion with the NOI he exercised a common ecumenism. His training assistant and hype man Drew Bundini Brown had found solace in Reformed Judaism, Angelo Dundee his trainer was Roman Catholic, and his beloved mother continued to be a Black Baptist. When Ali died, he was a global Muslim. He came to terms with his faith and reconciled that his mother and friends all shared hope and aspirations for a good life of freedom, prosperity, and a loving community. The world appreciated his charisma, physical prowess, and moral courage to live out his faith. The international outpouring was a loving spectacle to behold. People globally recognized him as one of the greatest.

# 4

# "A religious conversion, more or less": Eldridge Cleaver

The year 1977 was a momentous year: Ethel Waters died, I discovered Mary Lou Williams, and Muhammad Ali starred in the film *The Greatest* based on his best-selling autobiography. Jimmy Carter, a Southern evangelical, was days away from being inaugurated as the thirty-ninth president of the United States when I read T. D. Allman's article "The Rebirth of Eldridge Cleaver" in *The New York Times Magazine*.[1] Allman, a historian and a journalist, questioned whether Eldridge Cleaver, the once radical Black Panther, had become an opportunist by virtue of his evangelical conversion and a proponent of the "American Dream" instead of a righteous critic of the American state.[2]

Reading the article fascinated me. I was a junior in college thinking about how my religious upbringing could form into a coherent framework for addressing societal contradictions along the lines of race and class and more existentially questions of life and death. Like so many young people I had made an evangelical turn while in high school. This turn was made as I transitioned from New Orleans to Chicago as a teenager. I had left the comfort of my home congregation where I was schooled in the confessional/catechetical theology of the Missouri-Synod Lutherans. My Missouri-Synod Lutheran Church was one of those spaces where German Reformation theology met

American Negroes in a most interesting encounter of bourgeois aspirations and the politics of respectability. There I learned Luther's *Smaller Catechism* and the Augsburg Confession, written in 1530 and included in *The Book of Concord* that stemmed from Martin Luther's theological rebellious writings against Rome that prompted wars throughout Europe. The confession laid out the doctrinal operating principles of what was called Lutheranism. The confessional teachings and the Pauline Epistles were central to the church's claims regarding human freedom and God's grace. At the time, what attracted me to evangelicalism was its relational qualities. As a teenager, I was in need of good relationships living in a new city. My upstairs neighbors were two young Black men, whose stepfather was a White clergyman and an evangelical theologian, and they were my first friends in a new city. I found myself intrigued by my neighbor Ronald Behm's book with his co-author Columbus Salley, titled *Your God is Too White*. As I discovered new friends I also faced thorny issues of race from an evangelical theological lens. My youthful faith journey in a sense married a rationalistic Lutheran piety to an emotive American evangelicalism. At the time, I learned about Eldridge's turn to evangelicalism; I was thinking about, even preoccupied with, the fate of my own faith.

In the 1970s, evangelicalism was a rave, whether left or right—*Sojourners Magazine* on the left, Pat Robertson's Christian Broadcasting Network and Jerry Falwell's Moral Majority on the right. Even Stevie Wonder responded to this era. In two songs, "Higher Ground" and "Jesus Children in America" Wonder critically assessed the strengths and limitations of the American evangelicalism on his 1973 critically acclaimed album *Innervisions*. The album's signature song "Higher Ground" posed Wonder's wider concern for urban social deterioration, false social conscientiousness, and the Vietnam War:

People keep on learnin'
Soldiers keep on warrin'
World keep on turnin'
'Cause it won't be too long

The other song, "Jesus Children in America," provocatively questions the Jesus-talk of the early 1970s that pervaded both print and television mediums:

Hello Jesus

Hello children Jesus loves you of America

Are you hearing

What he's saying?[3]

Looking back on this transitory phase in my life I was open to a new religious experience. In this transitory phase of my life my neighbors invited me to a Tom Skinner rally at the Moody Bible Church where I was moved to openly acknowledge that I was a follower of Jesus. Skinner had modeled himself off Graham and he used his status as a former street gang member to build his reputation as authentically Black. Skinner published a number of books, which were more like pamphlets: *Black and Free* (1968); *How Black is the Gospel* (1970); *Words of Revolution* (1970); and *If Christ is the Answer, What Are the Questions?* (1974). Skinner, along with a host of others like Fuller Seminary's Dr. William Pannell, Dr. Ruth Bentley, and her husband Bill Bentley who headed the National Black Evangelical Association, valiantly attempted to answer Black Power Movement secularism and NOI religious nationalism theologically. For a very brief period, Skinner was like Graham in Black communities; he had rock star status and influenced a wide swath of Black urban adolescents including me. By the time I got to college I was questioning the evangelical paradigm of a simple relationship with Jesus. Alongside the Bible I read *Muhammad Speaks*, *The Black Panther*, and Black literature of all stripes. And on the wall of my room I had posters of Angela Davis, Huey Newton, Pam Grier, Jesus as a wanted revolutionary and a Black light zodiac sex astrology. It was a wonderfully rich, intellectually stimulating, and confusing time.

I had a hard time putting my finger on the intellectual problem then, but I had a feeling that things were not adding up. It took me years of thinking and writing to identify the discrepancies in the faith to which I had been exposed. Black evangelical theology was replete with the same individualism that plagued American evangelicalism more generally. As I saw it, evangelical pietism had a great deal to offer in terms of personal devotional habits, but it was never fully satisfactory in addressing perplexing questions of suffering and matters of structural inequities. To focus solely on individual sin was not a sufficient answer for me. It took me a while to figure out how American evangelicalism was one root of American individualism. In 1830, the French cultural observer of the United States, Alexis de Tocqueville, never fully understood American mores because he never fully got the country's evangelical heritage. He was an elite Catholic, culturally. Evangelicalism was foundational to American social behavior—abolitionist, slave, and slaver alike. God loved the person and the things of the person including sacrosanct personal property. This meant that Americans were more predisposed to the gospel according to seventeenth-century John Locke than the gospels written about the first-century Jesus. The Puritans' children had been more persuaded by sentiments of the colonial preacher Jonathan Edwards, who preached individual conversion, than the idea of living up to a communal covenant. Ralph Waldo Emerson's essay *Self-Reliance* was fueled by the Edwards' oxygen. What did Emerson say? "Trust thyself: every heart vibrates to that iron string. Accept the place the divine providence has found for you, the society of your contemporaries, the connection of events." Emerson sought to escape the heaviness of Calvinism with its burdens of sinfulness and election. It would be replaced by the more popular Methodism that enshrined an American spiritual perfectionism. Dour Calvinist with your dusty rules and reasoned confessions, move aside!

John Wesley, one of the English founders of Methodism, has as much to do with shaping the US ideology as anyone. He attempted to bring theological solace to the working poor in cities from London to Savannah in an era of gross inequities. Methodism attempted to be a comfort for those facing the most extreme form of labor exploitations, slavery, and concentrated wealth as industrial capitalism emerged. The economically conjoined twins of capitalism and racism brutalized lives across the Atlantic triangle from Africa, the Americas, and Europe. Amid this Wesley and his brother taught a spiritual method to assist the slowly industrializing working class and the agrarian dispossessed in a brutish world. Unlike the French Jean Calvin, who got stuck on election to prove that there was a monarchial sovereign God, Wesley informed his believers that God's grace, free action of love toward all humans, could help them to love as God loved them. They could overcome the brutish with an unyielding grace. It was noble. In Wesleyan theology God's love divinely infused each person. One need not prove one's worth; only a good God could do that. This led to conversion. Conversion meant one recognized one's sinfulness. This recognition was the beginning of true conversion, turning around from total self-centered and self-defeating behavior. Now here was the rub. The turnaround in Methodism was nearly always directed toward individual bad behavior—drunkenness, sex outside of marriage, and greed. Bad behavior could be easily sentimentalized as bad persons—Ebenezer Scrooge to Simon Legree. Of course, Wesley differed from Calvin; the latter based his theological ideation on the collective, a covenant, whereas the former focused strongly on individual behavior. Though Wesley claimed all actions began with God, his doctrine was quickly turned into a kind of American moral perfectionism. The notion of sanctification was popularly bastardized and became a kind of justification of a kind of moral purity. Well-behaved people are the saved. Let me offer, I do not wish to insult Methodism by being reductionist. My point is that the emphasis on born again Christian conversion language and perfectionism shaped the culture of the United States and is continuously used in today's self-help books.

Methodist ideas wove itself into the fabric of American civil religion. So, it should come as no surprise that Eldridge's family were staunch Methodists. Eldridge, the once angry Black man, whose anger challenged the goodness of the state, could become "good" again by converting to the right kind of citizen, and by showing respect to the institutions that were violently used to contain Black America. If God could change Eldridge, what might he do for the rest of Black America? This was the logic.

Though I found evangelicalism engaging, its inconsistencies forced me to think more deeply. The absence of social teachings in my formative exposure to Lutheranism and American evangelicalism became as challenging to me as Frederick Douglass found William Lloyd Garrison's idea that moral suasion alone could dismantle American slavery. As I wrestled with my own faith I developed a religious canon of readings that included Martin Luther King, Jr.'s *The Strength to Love*, Thomas Merton's *Seven Story Mountain*, German Dietrich Bonheoffer's *The Cost of Discipleship*, Benjamin Mays's memoir *Born to Rebel*, Howard Thurman's *Jesus and the Disinherited*, and the liberal theologian James Cone on *Black theology*. I used these readings to contrast them with Skinner and the American evangelical hero, Oxford University literary critic, and Christian apologist, C. S. Lewis, whose book *Mere Christianity* was the rage.[4] Lewis, the British patron saint of American evangelicals, took an approach to defending Christianity as a reasonable faith that did not address the troubling aspects of Christian histories in relation to the transatlantic slave trade and its residual histories. The spiritual needs of oppressed people or, as Howard Thurman phrased it, "the people with their backs against the wall" was a blind spot for a pious upper-class British man who benefited from Great Britain's exploits in Africa, Asia, and Australia. Living the life of an Oxford don had its privileges.

## "The Rebirth of Eldridge Cleaver"

This had been my youthful journey when I read in 1977 Allman's article on Eldridge. Allman was right to be skeptical of Eldridge's conversion. The context of Allman's skepticism needed to be broadened. Eldridge got the cultural moment. It was *America's Born-Again Years* to use historian Steven Miller's apt title. In 1975, Eldridge returned from his six year exile. Meanwhile his fellow Black Californian, Andre Crouch, and the Disciple gospel band chartered "Through it All" as Detroit's William "Smokey" Robinson crooned "Tracks of My Tears," and Parliament's anthem "Chocolate City" affirmed Black urban power. The legacy of the Great Migration left its own tracks of tears. Tears born out of conflict, frustrations, hopes, and social retrenchments. This is why Crouch sang "through it all."

There were different paths to Black liberation in Black communities. The Black Panther Party (BPP) was one expression. And then there was Jesus. The Jesus people made music and it flowed. It was both secular and religious performed by Sly and the Family Stone, the Edwin Hawkins Singers, Billy Preston, and Andraé Crouch. If the BPP called for a Ten-Point political platform, Sly sang "A Simple Song" and the Hawkins created vocal chords and octave changes on "Oh Happy Day" that were liberating too. The music and politics were born from the same struggles and heartaches—the same ones that Eldridge's family faced trekking from Arkansas to California, replete with competing ideas for Black advancement. One could not expect Allman to fully comprehend these streams of politics and faith. He could only offer skepticism, not a full analysis of why Eldridge chose to speak an evangelical language.

In 1975, Kathleen Cleaver in the *Los Angeles Times* began laying out the case for why Eldridge returned back to the United States. Watergate had undermined the Nixon administration and Ronald Reagan was no longer governor of California. This post-Watergate shift in politics gave Eldridge a better than even chance of receiving a fair hearing as a parolee. She opined, "Eldridge Cleaver has shown that he is a man of action. Every political philosophy he has embraced has been translated into action. Not only did he believe, but he attempted to implement his beliefs, under conditions in which many a more prudent person would have chosen to remain silent."[5] Her assessment of Cleaver as a man of action was on target. He was coming back to the United States as more seasoned and wiser in his politics after having been forced out of the BPP.

Bayard Rustin, the organizer of the march on Washington, brought his considerable skills as chair of the Eldridge Cleaver Defense Committee. His willingness to do so stemmed from his relationship to Kathleen; in addition to their progressive politics both had Quaker roots, hers from her boarding school days and his from his childhood community in Pennsylvania. Bayard's Quaker spirituality guided him in defending Eldridge. Despite being an openly same sex–loving male, Bayard courageously stood by Eldridge even though the latter had written some of the most injurious words about same sex–loving Black men when he targeted James Baldwin. In coming to Eldridge's defense, Bayard applied the same razor-sharp criticism he used when he exposed the limitations of Malcolm X's Black religious nationalism in a 1960 Harlem debate. Fearlessness, confession, and forgiveness of sin was a large part of Bayard's motivation. He also sympathetically reread his own fraught history as a former communist into Eldridge's case. In a 1976 press release he explained:

> It was not so surprising that Cleaver became disillusioned with Communism but that he neither abandoned politics nor turned to an opposite and equally-as-extreme doctrine was to me an indication that his thinking had reached an impressive degree of maturity. Cleaver remains a critic of injustice in America, but he insists that change must be democratic reform, not revolution. It has not been easy to raise money for Cleaver or to get people to join the committee. Images die-hard and for many the image of Cleaver as a hate-spewing revolutionary is so firmly etched in their minds that they are unable to see a new reality. Some leaders in the Black community are simply unable to forget or forgive Cleaver's abusive and unfair attacks of the past, attacks which he has now repudiated. And, as in the case of the biblical prodigal son there are those who resent Cleaver's change of heart and say why wasn't he with us back then.[6]

Bayard's defense of Eldridge resided in a hope that he might use his considerable talents as a writer and political celebrity to address American antidemocratic injustices. Additionally, and wishfully, he wanted Eldridge to bring his considerable experience of having traveled and lived in communist-governed countries to help bring to an end to American students' youthful infatuation with them. Bayard unwittingly imputed to Eldridge his own change of heart regarding communism during his youthful days in the 1930s. He criticized both the Black left and the White left for abandoning Eldridge. He was especially critical of White liberals for abandoning him after promoting him as a cause célèbre. His criticisms were not fully fair. However, the truths about Eldridge, the prodigal son, were more complicated than Bayard imagined.

## Soul on Ice

Eldridge had lived the life of an incarcerated man with all its ghosts. His story is one of many, too many, imprisoned Americans. Unjust and prolong incarceration has been a tool of the state and states since before the Civil War—juveniles, free person of color, and bound laborers experienced and witnessed those out-of-the-way spaces of correction. After slavery's demise, incarceration was increasingly used to control, intimidate, and subdue Black-laboring populations of men and women via nefarious legalisms—legalisms that in the twentieth century were justified by eugenics—genetic traits, cranial size, finger prints, all positing an explanation for why a group was disproportionately imprisoned.[7] It is a story that reaches into the entrails of American nationalism.[8] Men and women who had experienced these places of corrections outside of public scrutiny needed to tell their stories and make sense of their lives.

Eldridge's *Soul on Ice* was a part of a literary corpus that can be traced to Chester Himes in 1930s. Stories of incarcerated Black men have always been written in the forms of letters, self-published booklets, and oral histories, but none of it came to public awareness en masse until 1965 with the posthumously published book, *Autobiography of Malcolm X*. Malcolm's chapter on his incarceration is compelling. Prison monotony gave him plenty of time to think and educate himself. Looking inward, he found a faith in the Honorable Elijah Muhammad's preachments. This faith reclaimed his humanity. And Malcolm testified to his reclamation at Harlem street rallies, in the NOI temples of Philadelphia and New York and it was shared throughout prisons. Elijah Muhammad's ingenious proselytization strategy to the Black poor, specifically Black male prisoners, presented and used Malcolm as a star witness and example. It was as effective as John Wesley's.

Malcolm's journey—his charisma, sharp-witted and studied oratory— intellectually and spiritually became an inspiration for Eldridge. Malcolm's testimonies uttered in the name of Elijah Muhammad traveled through messaging systems of penitentiaries across the United States. Like Malcolm X, Eldridge followed suit and became a Muslim via the NOI. His need to read and write was so important to him that he conformed his behavior and became a model prisoner. In Soledad Prison, he was placed on the honor block. The honor block became more like a monastic cell with a door than a barred cell that lacked privacy. He could be at peace and find tranquility with his typewriter.[9]

In May 1965, Eldridge began correspondence with Constitutional trial lawyer Beverly Axelrod seeking her advice on how to publish his manuscript tentatively titled *White Woman, Black Man*.[10] He explained to Axelrod that he had been incarcerated for eight years and that he took up writing early in his confinement as "an emotional outlet for self-expression, dabbling around with poetry, essays, and short stories etc."[11] Eldridge went onto confide that the prison's censorship of his writing began with his NOI affiliation. His prison experience was a precursor to what would happen to Muhammad Ali publicly. "My present difficulty with the prison censorship," he observed, tracked back to 1960, when he was incarcerated in San Quentin. "I became a member of the Black Muslims. . . . In those days Islam as taught by Elijah Muhammad was receiving its first national publicity and it possessed, for people like myself—the ghettoites, the latent revolutionaries, the discontented, etc., . . . an irresistible attraction." He put his own affinity toward the NOI in context.

> I like to think of those years as the Years of Challenge, durring [sic] which America was challenged by black racism and white racism to take an irrevocable stand on what kind of nation we are going to have. It was made clear to me that all the blacks would no longer accept the quasi-servitude of the status quo and as a part of the Challenge to America, the Black Muslims offered to the blacks the dialectical opposite of Integration—Separation.

Eldridge's observation continued, "Well prison being what it is, all the forces in America are telescoped and magnified in prison in such a way as to compose an America in miniature."[12] The tenets of the NOI were more political than religious. Eldridge was never fully convinced by them.

Spiritually speaking, Eldridge was in continuity with a longer American history. The religious historian Leigh Schmidt in his book *Restless Souls: The Making of American Spirituality* describes in the main how wealthy White Protestants searched for spirituality outside of American Protestantism.[13] The irony of this search for spirituality was that it was actually in a continuum with the search for an emotive faith that traces itself back to the evangelical break from the formalist weight of Calvinist teachings. What was different about Eldridge's search was that it came from an incarcerated Black American writer challenging societal long-practiced injustices and long-held sexual taboos. His questions concerning faith were interlaced with transcendental issues about racism, democracy, political power, maleness, and sexualities.

When the manuscript, *White Woman, Black Man,* was published as *Soul on Ice* in 1968, the editor got the title right. The book was the complicated search of an imprisoned Black man trying to make sense of a variety of existential confusions. The titled hearkened back to the W. E. B. DuBois's *Souls of Black Folk.*

DuBois's preface to *Souls* depicted Black America as a warring self. He detected the twoness of Black life living in a dominant White world. The power imbalance meant that Black people as the weaker party were always scorned and seen as "a problem." Therefore, the Black self was not liberated to act freely on its own accord. Black folk were under constant surveillance and dictated to through a dial controlled by White cultural tastemakers. This constant state of bifurcation that continuously dogged Black life tore it asunder according to DuBois. If this was true of Black collectivity, this was truer for Eldridge who lived being daily probed and microscopically observed. Before American academic fandom for the late French scholar Michel Foucault, author of the seminal work on prisons, *Discipline and Punish*, Eldridge had lived in the prisoners' panopticon. *Soul on Ice* was an apropos title. The book attempted to make sense of his journey, including his personal desires and his country's structural inconsistencies while under lock and key.

My initial foray into *Soul on Ice* was as a teenager. The Black Arts Movement, the artistic extension of the Black Power, and the American evangelical reawakening weren't disparate. They arose alongside of each other and were intertwined. Reading the literary anthology *Black Voices* was connected to my thinking about Jesus, as much as it was to the immediate aftermath of the assassinations of Martin Luther King, Jr., Mark Clark, and Fred Hampton, and to the trials of Bobby Seale and Angela Davis. My initial reading of *Soul on Ice* reflected my own concern about incarceration. In my New Orleans childhood, the Louisiana prison plantation, Angola, loomed large as well as the juvenile reformatory in Scotlandville that seemed as frighteningly heinous as the state penitentiary. I was keenly aware of ex-convicts in my community and the assaults that were done to their bodies and souls. I think every child who was linked to New Orleans working-class life knew to dread the Louisiana State Penitentiary. R&B recording artist Aaron Neville expressed the fear lyrically in *Angola Bound* "You come up here skippin' an 'a jumpin', oh/Lord it won't last long/Gonna wish you was a baby boy, in your mother's arms." So, I read

Eldridge's book, just as I read *Soledad Brother: Prison Letters of George Jackson*, because I knew women and men who were or had been incarcerated. What I missed in my first readings of *Soul on Ice* was how much of discussion there was about faith. It was a constant theme throughout the book's vignettes.

In 1997, *The Oxford Companion to African American Literature* broke down the book thematically this way:

> "Letters from Prison," describing Cleaver's experiences with and thoughts on crime and prisons.
>
> "Blood of the Beast," discussing race relations and promoting black liberation ideology.
>
> "Prelude to Love—Three Letters," Two love letters written to Cleaver's attorney, Beverly Axelrod and one written to Cleaver by Axelrod.
>
> "White Woman, Black Man," on gender relations, black masculinity, and sexuality.[14]

These were big themes, but the critics were not sensitive enough to the fact that Eldridge was commenting on the kind of faith that had guided Black people, Islam, and Christianity. Throughout *Soul* Eldridge offered an extended commentary on his own faith or lack thereof as much as the literary themes my esteemed colleagues outlined. If the prison was American in miniature, the themes of faith were also in play.

David Hilliard, the former chief of Staff of the BPP, recollected meeting Eldridge in 1966. Hilliard observed that he was "the personification of Malcolm X."[15] X, lest we forget, was the personification of Black religious nationalism. That is, his call for Black America's transformation was based on a religious understanding. Too often contemporary scholars including Malcolm X's major biographer the late Manning Marable submerge religion as though it was not the principal driver of his activism. Whether or not we like it or share it, much of X's activism came out his concern for Black lives as spiritual people. Eldridge, also, very much understood that the inner self was crucial. This is why he spent a fair amount of time in *Soul on Ice* observing it and its ethical consequences. Religion was important to transforming the inner self.

In his opening salvo in *Soul* he described a numb life. He wrote that "Novocain," the pain-numbing medication, had worn off. He was arrested and incarcerated for selling marijuana in junior high school and was sent to penitentiary in 1954. In prison, so he claims, he became an atheist the more he grew aware of his political fate. He penned:

> While all this was going on, our group was espousing atheism. Unsophisticated and not based on any philosophical rationale, our atheism was pragmatic. I had come to believe that there is no God; if there is, men do not know anything about him. Therefore, all religions were phony— which made all preachers and priests, in our eyes, fakers, including the ones scurrying around the prison who, curiously, could put in a good word for you with the Almighty Creator of the universe but could not get anything down with the warden or parole board—they could usher you through the Pearly Gates *after you were dead*, but through the prison gate *while you were still alive and kicking*. Besides, men of the cloth who work in prison have an ineradicable stigma attached to them in the eyes of convicts because they escort condemned men into the gas chamber. Our atheism was a source of enormous pride to me. Later on, I bolstered our arguments by reading Thomas Paine and his devastating critique of Christianity in particular and organized religion in general.[16] (emphasis original)

Eldridge, the iconoclast, questioned everything. "I attacked all forms of piety, loyalty, and sentiment: marriage, love, God, patriotism, the Constitution, the founding fathers, law, concepts of right-wrong-good-evil, all forms of ritualized and conventional behavior." He, horrifyingly, broke all moral strictures. "I became a law unto myself—my own legislature, my own supreme court, my own executive." His narcissistic delusion led him to becoming a rapist. Eldridge confessed that he raped Black women first to hone his abilities as a rapist "across the tracks." In his mind, he sought to destroy White society's most prized possession: "white women." No matter his justification what he did was ruthlessly defile the human personhood of women. In short, he hated women.

Eldridge's powerful rage that justified in his own mind his rape of women was layered and complex. He was enraged at his own bisexual struggles. As a male prisoner, he loved men too. "It is important to realize," according to one author on prison sexuality, "that whether a Man is sexually involved or not, his status is sexually defined."[17] In Eldridge's papers collected at Texas A&M University is an unpublished novel, *Book of Lives*, written before *Soul on Ice*. It is a story of two male prisoners as complex lovers. It was Eldridge's version of *Giovanni's Room*, a novel written by James Baldwin in 1956. Baldwin's novel was of same-sex intimacy love and struggle and so was Eldridge's. Though the novel is stylized similarly to Baldwin's, I can only speculate whether much of it is real. Many males of Eldridge's generation appeared to hold fixed and rigid philosophies regarding sexual acts at least for appearances' sake. Unlike Ethel Waters, whose sexual marginalization as a woman paradoxically gave her sexual autonomy, a furtive freedom to love both women and men as she desired, Eldridge was an incarcerated male who lived in a world where sexual intimacy was more likely determined by dominant aggression. His masculinity aligned with the harsh realities of prison hierarchies. In other words, who was on top? Philosopher Tommy Curry analyzes Cleaver's *The Book of Lives* as a text of Black male disempowerment.[18] His conflicted relationships might have led to what he called his "nervous breakdown." The therapist who treated him "went Freudian," trying to get at his deepest fears about his mother. He resisted those inquiries. However, as a man in and out of prison custody, he had to deal with prison homosocialness, desire, and sexuality and what those things meant in terms of his own image of manhood. As a prisoner, perhaps one of his greatest fears was truly falling in love with another man.

Eldridge's infamous attack on James Baldwin's sexuality resided in his confused thoughts on homosocial intimacies as something repellent or dirty.

Rather than face his own conflicting desires as an incarcerated felon, Eldridge made wholesale generalizations regarding the two-faced posture of Black intellectuals. In his mind Baldwin was the Black intellect gone awry. He penned:

> The black homosexual, when his twist has a racial nexus, is an extreme embodiment of this contradiction. The white man has deprived him of his masculinity, castrated him in the center of his burning skull, and when he submits to this change and take the white for his lover as Big Daddy, he focuses on "whiteness" all the love in his pent-up soul and turns the razor edge of hatred against "blackness"—upon himself, what he is, and all those who look like him, remind him of himself. He may even hate the darkness of night. The racial death-wish is manifested as the driving force in James Baldwin. His hatred for blacks, even as he pleads what he conceives as their cause, makes him the apotheosis of the black bourgeoisie who have completely rejected their African heritage, consider the loss irrevocable, and refuse to look again in that direction.[19]

Though Eldridge never explicitly stated it, one senses by reading between the lines that Baldwin's audacious mannerism and physical stature reminded him of the prison punk.[20] Eldridge was a man steeped in prison masculinity. He noted that "Baldwin's essay on Richard Wright reveals that he despised—not Richard Wright—but his masculinity. He cannot confront the stud in others—except that he must submit to it or destroy it."[21] His intimate dissonances did not prevent him from holding a certain kind of notion of what manhood meant. Instead of thinking through his perceptions he succumbed to the angry rhetoric of prison masculinity in criticizing Baldwin.[22] However, the heated hyperbole of his pen hid perhaps his own clashing desires. In reality, he was performing the same intellectual contortionist act that he had critiqued other Black intellectuals of doing. And in the end, he was trying to, figuratively speaking, kill "father" Baldwin, just as Baldwin had once attempted to kill his writing "father" Richard Wright.

And these same clashes found their way into his initial forays regarding his thoughts on religion. *The Book of Lives* was as much about religion as it was about sexuality; the chief character is named "Little Jesus," and the plot takes place around the prison chapel.[23] Religions circumscribed and defined the etiquettes of human sexuality. They served as a guide to ethical boundaries for who should be loved spiritually and physically. In ancient thought among elite Greeks the male body and same-sex love were held in high praise, though physically and sexually abused slaves were simply referred to as barbarians. The Apostle Paul preached an apocalyptic celibacy and was mortified that Rome forced slaves into temple prostitution. The further point here is that Eldridge began exploring religion in prison as he tried to figure his own intimate relations in a setting of power dynamics. In my mind, if Eldridge raped women outside of prison there is nothing to preclude his rape of males inside of prison. But when he became a Muslim he had to shun same-sex practices of prison life. His confusion and desires led him to try to figure out his identity. His salvation came through writing.

"In the beginning was the word," according to the Gospel of John, and Eldridge found the word. This should not come as a surprise: the Abrahamic texts from the Torah and Psalms, the Christian New Testament, and the Quran are filled with beautifully devised poems, hymns, and lesson-filled stories of faith. In an eloquent passage Eldridge writes, "This is why I started to write to save myself. I realized that no one could save me but myself." Eldridge understood that "prison authorities were both uninterested and unable to help me. I had to seek out the truth and unravel the snarled web of my motivations." He declared: "I had to find out who I am and what I could do to become the best of which I was capable. I understood that what happened to me had also happened to countless other Blacks and it would happen to many, many more."[24] Writing was Eldridge's way of ordering his life. It was a way of linking his own self-awareness to the broader social movements that challenged structures of belonging and citizenship in the United States. "That is why I decided to concentrate on my writings and efforts in this area." He opined, "We are a very sick country—I, perhaps, sicker than most. But I accept that. I told you in the beginning that I am extremist by nature—so it, is only right that I should be extremely sick."[25] Here metaphorically speaking was his Pauline self-conflict, "I do not understand my own actions. For I do not do what I want, but I do the very thing I hate" (Rom. 7:15 NRSV).

Eldridge's self-reconciliation began first with deciding on his political faith. Joining the NOI under Malcolm X's tutelage led him to a positive faith in Black people's power to organize themselves into a coherent family. And in his mind families were run by men. This is why NOI's religious unification appealed to him. Eldridge also found their emphasis on self-reliance traceable back to his family's Black Arkansan heritage. The NOI affirmed ideological notions he heard in his childhood rearing about manhood. Central to the success of the NOI was Elijah and Clara Muhammad's experience as Black Southerners. Their conservatism appealed to the denizens of the Great Migration, their ferocious longing for self-autonomy, economic independence, and collective self-governance, which were quintessentially American. And it was Malcolm's vivid NOI proselytization that captured these aspirations and put them defiantly into words that captured Eldridge and turned him into one of the faithful.

When Malcolm was assassinated, Eldridge, like so many others, was devastated. His faith in the NOI died. For Eldridge, the "Black Muslim movement was destroyed the moment Elijah cracked the whip over Malcolm's head, because it was not the Black Muslim movement itself that was so irresistibly appealing to true believers," but Malcolm. Malcolm, he believed, helped awaken "twenty million Negroes" to self-consciousness. He was compelling. "When he spoke under the banner of Elijah Muhammad he was irresistible," Eldridge wrote ecstatically. "When he spoke under his own banner he was still irresistible." Passionately he notes, "If he had become a Quaker, a Catholic, or a Seventh-Day Adventist, or a Sammy Davis-style Jew, and if he had continued to give voice to the mute ambitions in the Black man's soul, his message would still have been triumphant because what was great was not Malcolm X but the truth he uttered."[26]

In Eldridge's mind Malcolm's religious appeal was about the power to resurrect the Black masses from the dead. Malcolm represented a redeemed Black masculinity. For him Malcolm embodied manhood at its best. "Every institution is tainted by the mystique of race," he wrote, "and the question of masculinity is confused by the presence of both a *white* man and a *black* man here." The racial relationship between males left the United States discombobulated. Echoing the eighteenth-century philosopher Hegel he observed,

> One was the master and the other was the slave until a moment ago when they both were declared equal *men*; which leaves American men literally without a unitary, nationally viable self-image. Whatever dim vision of masculinity they have a rough-and-ready, savage mishmash of violence and sexuality, dichotomized exercise and worship of physical force/submission to fear of physical force—which is only one aspect of the broken-down relationship between men and women in America.[27]

This struggle of who would be on top would be reflected in constant tropes throughout his life.

The energy he drew from Malcolm and the NOI was in terms of a spirituality of male assertiveness. He likened Black history to Elijah Muhammad's interpretation of the Christian New Testament parable of Lazarus.

> The New Testament parable of Jesus raising Lazarus from the dead is interpreted by the Black Muslims as a symbolic parallel to the history of Negro America. By capturing black men in Africa and bringing them to slavery in America, the white devils *killed* the black man—killed him mentally, culturally spiritually, economically, politically, and morally—transforming

him into *a Negro*, the symbolic Lazarus left to the *graveyard* of segregation and second-class citizenship.

For him, Elijah Muhammad and Malcolm played a role similar to Jesus in being "summoned by God to lift the modern Lazarus, the Negro, from his grave."[28] To Eldridge the Muhammad Ali–Floyd Patterson first championship bout was symbolic of liberated manhood. Colorfully, he expressed his political theology of manliness by writing the following:

> The America out of which Elijah Muhammad calls his people is indeed doomed, crumbling, burning, if not by the hand of God then by the hand of man, and this doomed America was partly buried in the boxing ring at Las Vegas when Muhammad Ali pounded a die-hard Lazarus into submission. With the America that is disappearing, the Lazarus-man created in the crucible of its hatred and pain is also vanishing. The victory of Muhammad Ali over Floyd Patterson marks the victory of a New World over an Old World, of life and light over Lazarus and the darkness of the grave. This is America recreating itself out of its own ruins. The pain is mighty for every American, black or white, because the task is gigantic and by no means certain of fulfillment. But there are strong men in the land and they will not be denied. Their task will not be ended until Paul Bunyan and John Henry can look upon themselves and each other as men, the strength in the image of the one not being at the expense of the other.[29]

He wondered as well as worried: who would call the people back to life after Malcolm's assassination? His faith had been placed in charismatic masculinity to redeem Black communities.

It was during Eldridge's early years of incarceration that he developed a pattern of exploring hierarchical male-headed organizations. His first was Roman Catholicism. In his youth while incarcerated in a California Youth Authority facility he became a Catholic. "Once I was a Catholic. I was baptized, made my first Communion, my Confirmation, and I wore a Cross with Jesus on my neck." We often forget that young people as a part of growing up and rebellion try on faith. For some it is faddish, for others it becomes an ongoing lived reality. Although he does not discuss how long he remained a Catholic, one gets the sense that he was meaningfully trying to live up to its disciplines. "I prayed at night, said my Rosary, went to Confession, and said all the Hail Marys and Our Fathers to which I was sentenced by the priest."[30] This was in the 1950s. And though he did not realize it gave him a connectedness with both Mary Lou Williams and Floyd Patterson, the same Patterson whom he unmercifully criticized. Eldridge downplayed why he became a Catholic. He reduced his attachment solely to the ethno-racial stratification of the youth facility. "The reason I became a Catholic was that the rule of the institution held that every Sunday each inmate had to attend the church of choice. I chose the Catholic Church because all the Negroes and Mexicans went there." The youth facility bounded racialized European Reformation structure. "The whites went to the Protestant chapel. Had I been a fool enough to go to the Protestant chapel, one black face in a sea of white, and with guerilla warfare going on between us, I might have ended up a Christian martyr—St. Eldridge the Stupe."[31] I have no doubt regarding the truth behind his statement and the intra-prison conflicts, but his description is not sufficient given his enthusiasm and willingness to conform to the church's discipline. Problematically, the priest in charge silenced an inquiring young Black man.

> It all ended one day when at catechism class, the priest asked if anyone present understood the mystery of the Holy Trinity. I had been studying my lessons diligently and knew by heart what I'd been taught. Up shot my hand, my heart throbbing with piety (pride) for this chance to demonstrate my knowledge of the Word. To my great shock and embarrassment, the Father announced, and it sounded like a thunderclap, that I was lying, that no one, not even the Pope, understood the Godhead and why else did I think they called it the *mystery* of the Holy Trinity? I saw in a flash, stung to the quick jeers of my fellow catechumens, that I had been used, that the Father had

been lying in wait for the chance to drop that thunderbolt, in order to drive home the point that the Holy Trinity was not to be taken lightly.[32]

In a youth facility, the priest was a gatekeeper and slamming a bright young man kept others from asking questions. Eldridge humorously wrote, "I had intended to explain the Trinity with an analogy to 3-in-1 oil so it was probably just as well."[33] Though he ended this vignette with lightheartedness I have no doubt that this act of cruelty cut more deeply than he let on. It was so hurtful he bookmarked it.

Eldridge also encountered a more influential teacher over the course of his confinement, Chris Lovdjieff. He nicknamed Lovdjieff "The Christ" for his singular dedication to teaching and enlightening prisoners. "Chris Lovdjieff had a profound and an ecumenical education. . . . It was as he had seen or experienced something which had changed him forever, sickened his soul, overwhelmed with sympathy, and love for mankind."[34] Lovdjieff fashioned himself to be a disciple of Alan W. Watts, who occasionally came to "Q," as Eldridge referred to San Quentin, to teach. Watts was an upper-class Englishman who moved to the United States and eventually to California after leaving the Episcopal priesthood as a devotee of D. T. Suzuki who popularized Zen Buddhism to Americans. Watts was, so to speak, Suzuki's White male interpreter and was popularly hailed in periodicals.[35] Eldridge felt Watts was more gloss than substance. He was like "a slick advertisement for a labor-saving device, aimed at the American housewife, out of the center of *Life* magazine," he assessed.[36] He judged Lovdjieff as being more wise, humane, and smarter than Watts. Watts was interesting, but not enough to attract Eldridge to Eastern religions.

The most important person that Lovdjieff brought into Eldridge's purview was the Catholic Trappist monk Thomas Merton. Eldridge was simultaneously disgusted by and attracted to Merton, perhaps in the same way he was attracted to being a Catholic in the California juvenile detention facility. I can only surmise that he never completely discarded his attraction to the mass as a dramatic rendering of the deep and unifying mystery of the transcendent oneness of human community. However, as he explained, it was Lovdjieff that promoted Merton. "He seemed desperately to want us to respect Merton's vocation and choice of the contemplative life," he offered. "It was an uphill battle because a prison is in many ways like a monastery." All prisoners hated being imprisoned and in disgust wondered why "a free man would voluntarily enter prison—or a monastery." Eldridge's initial reaction to Merton was that he "was some kind of nut." They thought this of Lovdjieff too. But what really disturbed Eldridge was his "secret disgust . . . that in many ways" he was himself a monk, a view he loathed of himself.[37]

Lovdjieff pleaded with Eldridge to read Merton. When in San Quentin Eldridge was placed in solitary confinement for his Black Muslim activism, he found time to read Merton's *Seven Story Mountain*, which was listed as one of the prison's acceptable books. "I was tortured by that book," he reacted, "because Merton's suffering in his quest for God, seemed all in vain to me." Cynically he penned, "At the time, I was a Black Muslim chained in the bottom of the pit by the Devil. . . . To me, the language and symbols of religion were nothing but weapons of war. I had no purpose for them."[38] Yet, something about Merton attracted him enough that he wished Merton had made a more secularly political argument for his decision to join a monastery. Something in Merton's prose was deeply arresting for him. "Despite my rejection of Merton's theistic world view, I could not keep him out of the room. He shouldered his way through the door." In solitary confinement's loneliness Eldridge finally relented: "Welcome, Brother Merton. I gave him a bear hug." Eldridge appreciated Merton's style, especially the way Merton used vivid prose to narrate his spiritual journey. Later, Merton's *Seven Story Mountain* served as the template for Eldridge's own spiritual memoir, *Soul on Fire*. Thomas Merton was a force in Eldridge's life.

Eldridge's links to Catholics and Catholicism did not end with his parole. His first job outside of prison was writing as a journalist for *Ramparts*, a little-known West Coast Catholic magazine that in its earliest days published Merton. The magazine initially started as a creative outlet for American Catholics, focusing on fiction, poetry, and prose. It was informed by Catholic social teachings in response to Pope John XXIII and the public theology of Martin Luther King, Jr. It quickly began to have writers that took on the traditional teachings of the church on controversial issues such as contraception. The magazine increasingly began to have a louder voice on social issues concerning the national civil rights movement, the presidential candidacy of Republican US Senator Barry Goldwater, and the escalating war in Vietnam. By 1965, the magazine's open challenge to bishops caused a financial backlash. The financial woes were such that the magazine chose to widen its editorial leadership ecumenically, inviting prominent Jews and Protestants to join such as lawyer, social activist, and Protestant theologian William Stringfellow, and Arthur Cohen, vice-president of Holt, Rinehart, and Winston. It was Beverly Axelrod, Eldridge's lawyer, who smuggled his writings out of prison and brought them to *Ramparts*. The magazine initially published some of his essays that served as the foundation of *Soul on Ice*. Upon his release from prison in late 1966, after serving nine of fourteen years in prison for rape, he joined the magazine as a writer. The magazine's ties were then still linked, though fragilely, to Catholic social teachings.[39] *Ramparts* took a risk on Eldridge given his past, a risk rooted in its liberal Catholic ethos. By the time Eldridge began writing for the magazine, *Ramparts* had made a full left turn as a muckraking investigative social justice periodical. By 1968, with the publication of *Soul on Ice*, Eldridge was a national celebrity.

Though Eldridge made claims to a kind of secularist ideology, his religious soul searching never was as distant and secular as he claimed. His inner self, his claims to humanity needed to express his spirituality in some form or fashion. In an extensive *Playboy* magazine interview done by the writer Nat Hentoff, Eldridge, at that time the Minister of Information of the BPP, forcefully stated the case for a disciplined revolutionary movement. In the interview, he paused to discuss his self-reflective journey just as he had done in *Soul on Ice*. He offered this commentary on his inhumanity as a rapist:

> I came to realize that the particular women I had victimized had not been involved in actively oppressing me or other black people. I was taking revenge on them for what the whole system was responsible for. And as I thought about it, I felt that I had become less than human. I also came to see that the price of hating other human beings is loving oneself less. But this didn't happen all at once: beginning to write was important part of getting myself together. In fact, looking back, I started to write to save myself.[40]

This interview was published just before Eldridge would flee the United States and go into exile in Cuba, a move prompted by a shoot-out between the Oakland police and the BPP in which he was involved. The shoot-out took place two days after the assassination of Martin Luther King, Jr., a context too often forgotten.

King's assassination enraged Eldridge. In fact, he left his desk at the magazine while writing an essay for *Ramparts* titled "The Death of Martin Luther King: Requiem for Nonviolence" to join his fellow Oakland BPP members. What followed was a murderous rampage in which a surrendering, gunless Bobby Hutton, the youngest and one of the first members to join the BPP, was killed by Oakland police. Eldridge never explicitly admitted to his grief as the motivating factor that led to the shoot-out with the police, but his incomplete essay left on his desk hours before the incident is an ode filled with homicidal anger and blinding anguish. Though he and the BPP disagreed with King's philosophy and nonviolent tactics, they respected that he aimed for Black liberation. He wrote that an "assassin's bullet not only killed Dr. King, it killed a period of history. It killed a hope, and a dream."[41] With King's death he warily penned, "It's all dead now. Now there is the gun and the bomb, dynamite and the knife, and they will be used liberally in America. America will bleed. America will suffer."[42]

## *Soul on Fire*

Eldridge's and his wife Kathleen's exile years were exciting and constantly difficult. Even though Eldridge was forced into exile, he and Kathleen continued to be popular icons. They were frequently photographed as the Black Power Movement's most notable couple, sought out by writers, journalists, and scholars. Though seen as celebrities, the Cleavers were also subject to the whims of the governments that hosted them. As BPP representatives they were often used to embarrass US government and position it as a racist colonial power. However, these same governments found the Cleavers expendable when it came to negotiating with the US government. Added to their vulnerability was the consistent harassment by US intelligence agencies abroad while domestically the FBI's COINTELPRO program successfully fomented antagonisms within the BPP. He had seen through his extensive travels to China, Cuba, Vietnam, the former Soviet Union, and parts of the African continent that Cold War politics and the revolutionary politics of emerging countries were equally hypocritical.

In addition, the years living in exile had strained the Cleaver's marital relationship. In the end, Eldridge was tired and dissatisfied with living in France after having lived in Algeria and before that Cuba. For Eldridge, being outside the country was too isolating ethnically and politically. He claimed that he did not want their eldest child growing up speaking French, but that was subterfuge. He wanted to return home. He wasn't alone. Other ex-patriots like North Carolina activist Robert Williams, who advocated self-defense for Black Americans years before the BPP with his seminal book *Negroes With Guns*, also returned back to the United States. Eldridge spoke about how he struggled in exile especially about his misadventures in Cuba to the scholar Henry Louis Gates Jr. in a 1976 interview in the magazine *Transition*.[43] He was repentant.

Making his decision to return to the United States, Eldridge understood that American conservatism had ascended both religiously and politically. In the 1970s, it was Billy Graham's America more than it was Martin Luther King Jr.'s America. In *Soul on Ice* he astutely questioned the binary politics of right and left. He wrote, "Whether America decisively moves to the right or to the left is the fundamental political problem in the world today; and the most serious question now before the American people is who now, in this post-civil rights era, are the true patriots, the new right or the new left?"[44] While abroad Eldridge read the tea leaves and decided to reconcile his personal fate and reinvent himself, faith-wise, in the evangelical mainstream. He was not unusual. Black conservatism was also ascending in other spaces as historian Angela Dillard in her important and too little recognized *Guess Who's Coming to Dinner Now? Multicultural Conservatism in America*. Dillard points out that American political conservatism had multiple minority faces.[45] We know that Cleaver revered Malcolm X, but so did Clarence Thomas. So, Eldridge's move from a Black religious nationalist to a secular Marxist to an evangelical patriot was not that far a stretch. The NOI represented a long conservative Black self-help tradition of doing for oneself and critiqued state liberalism for creating dependency. The BPP's Ten-Point Plan also called for community control and community independence. Eldridge's conservative political turning is not difficult to posit. He, like Muhammad Ali, endorsed Ronald Reagan for president in the 1980s. For Eldridge, this was not tricky because in 1968 when he wrote an open letter to then governor Reagan, he wrote BPP members' right to bear arms at the California state capital. His logic did not differ from Barry Goldwater, Arizona US Senator and 1964 Republican presidential nominee. He was making the same claims to individual liberties and freedoms.[46] Eldridge was consistent. In fact, he anticipated a global trend in religion and politics as he conjoined his political ideology to the evangelical fray. The decline of democratic liberal institutions via American Cold War machinations, as well as corruptly administered socialist governments, helped to create a massive political shift toward religiously informed politics beginning with the 1978 Iranian Revolution. Eldridge's move from a Black religious nationalist to a secularist BPP member to evangelical patriot was not completely faked as scholar Ashely Lavelle has argued.[47] It had continuity.

*Soul on Fire* was a fuller testimonial of his life than *Soul on Ice*. His template for writing it was *Seven Story Mountain*. Eldridge wrote of his journey and his familial hardship as part of the Great Migration's *Tracks of My Tears*. His family moved from Arkansas to Arizona to Southern California. In the book, he described his troubled relationship to the narrowness of Black evangelical life and his father.

Eldridge's maternal and paternal grandfathers were staunch Arkansas Methodists in the African Methodist Episcopal tradition. His grandfathers were cut from the Black self-help tradition found in so much of the ideology surrounding manhood—moral grounding in religion and an emphasis on property ownership and economic independence However, his father Leroy had no use for religion. "My Father," he wrote "had no patience for church going." His father was openly atheistic. "If you asked him," he continued, "he'd tell you in a minute, 'No. There ain't no God. And I am the only Santa Claus you ever gonna see.'"[48] He also wrote that his parents had a troubled relationship and were often at odds. Eldridge's father was abusive to his mother and beat her. His father knocked him unconscious for attempting to defend his mother during one of their fights. Their domestic struggles affected the entire family, and though Eldridge never attributed their hurt relationship to his own angry and troubled criminal decisions, his father undoubtedly had an impact on his later criminal life. Whatever the case psychologically, we know that Eldridge was adrift and torn by self-destructive behavior for a good portion of his life. Tragically, it was claimed that he battered Kathleen Cleaver the same way his father had battered his mother.[49] His moves toward faith, whether it was Catholicism, the NOI, the BPP, Evangelicalism, or Mormonism, were a search for some kind of moral grounding, however confused it appears.

Eldridge's seeking out of moral grounding does not preclude his political or economic calculations. Reading Eldridge's conversion narrative in *Soul on*

*Fire*, it is abundantly clear that he was aware of it as a literary trope stemming from his childhood Methodism. He wrote in dramatic fashion of his concerns for returning to the United States and the spiritual crisis it put him in. He storied the following:

> I returned to the Mediterranean Coast and began thinking of putting an end to it all by committing suicide. I really began to think about that. I was sitting up on my balcony, one night, on the thirteenth floor—just sitting there. It was a beautiful Mediterranean night—sky stars, moon hanging there in a sable void. I was brooding, downcast, at the end of my rope. I looked up at the moon and saw certain shadows . . . and saw certain shadows . . . and the shadows became a man in the moon, and I saw a profile of myself (a profile that we had used on posters for the Black Panther Party something I had seen a thousand times). I was already upset and this scared me. When I saw that image. I started trembling. It was a shaking that came from deep inside, and it had a threat about it that this mood was getting worse, that I could possibly disintegrate on the scene and fall apart. As I stared at this image, it changed and I was my former heroes paraded before my eyes. Here was Fidel Castro, Mao Tse-sung, Karl Marx, Frederick Engels, passing in review—each one appearing for a moment of time, and then dropping out of sight, like fallen heroes. Finally at the end of the procession, in dazzling shimmering light the image of Jesus Christ appeared. That was the last straw.[50]

He ended this extensive passage describing how he wept and found a Bible that had been substituted for *The Communist Manifesto* and *Das Kapital* and read the twenty-third Psalm. He then fell asleep, sleeping the soundest he had in years.

What is also intriguing was the fact that Eldridge published his second memoir with Word Books. Given his notoriety one would have thought that he might have published a memoir on a much larger national press, one that could have distributed more widely than Word. Word was better known for its religious recording business than as a publisher. Was Eldridge so calculating that he would turn down a more lucrative contract by a major publisher? Or did all the major publishers decide he was no longer in vogue? It could have been, but Eldridge more likely was betting on having a bestseller like Charles Colson, the special counsel to President Richard Nixon, who was convicted and served jail time for the infamous national disgrace in the Watergate Scandal. Colson's *Born Again* sold five million copies for Chosen Books, an evangelical publisher. In fact, Charles Colson wrote a blurb for *Soul on Fire*, legitimizing Eldridge in the evangelical world. However, Eldridge's *Soul on Fire* was not rewarded like *Soul on Ice*, which sold two million copies. Word was too small and they could not make their White evangelical base care enough about Eldridge as an important subject. They could not generate the publicity and wide reviews for the book. Colson fit the evangelical paradigm of a life worth reading about, not Eldridge.

Lastly, Eldridge hoped that joining up with the evangelicals would extend his celebrity. Evangelicals were stars—pop stars, politicians, preachers, singers, and actors. The star power of evangelicals in the 1970s owed itself to Billy Graham's worldwide rock star status. By the 1980s, Pat Robertson's Christian television station was quite formidable and evangelical shows abounded. Eldridge had been a star and he wanted to stay in the limelight even though his BPP days were over. The problem was he had no agent and his act was limited.

For White evangelicals Eldridge was a golden catch. He legitimized their program by being a former Black radical claimed by Jesus. He had a similar role as Ethel Waters, but he was, in their parlance, a much more notorious sinner as a radical who found the light. However, in spite of Eldridge's best efforts to up his new profile as an evangelical, it did not catch on with his true base in Black America. People seemed to not to trust him fully, even though *Soul on Fire* demonstrated masterful insights as much as *Soul on Ice*. He was seen as rightist and a betrayer of Black struggle in many quarters. And the new more professionalized class of Black conservatives were too busy attempting to curry favor in the Reagan administration and kept their distance from him, thinking him to be a convict turned conman.

A reality for Eldridge was economics. He was broke! He was without independent resources. He was as dependent on evangelical largesse as the Blacks that he criticized for being too dependent on state liberalism. As much as evangelicals lauded him, they did not reward him very handsomely, though they did offer him a decent paying writing job equivalent to the one he once had at *Ramparts*, with the major evangelical magazine *Christianity Today* that at the time had an entirely White staff. Though Eldridge went on the speaking tour in white evangelical congregations, he was not drawing speaking fees of the magnitude of Charles Colson. But he wasn't a Black version of Charles Colson.[51] His calculated gambit to align with conservative evangelicals did not pay off. When he returned back to the United States he had no money, and joining the evangelical lecture circuit did not yield him any money.

After his 1977 plea bargain where he escaped jail time for his participation in the 1968 shoot-out with the Oakland Police in return for community service, Eldridge had little money. He was simply another broke celebrity. In this moment, he joined the spiritual marketplace that Black men and women had used to build communities and receive remuneration historically.[52] But it was not easy to do what Clara and Elijah Muhammad had done building the NOI. First, he hooked up with a Sun Myung Moon's Unification Church outfit project volunteer. He then tried to organize his own church in Oakland, the Third Cross Church of the Holy Ghost. In 1980, he tried to form a hybrid religion from Christianity and Islam that he labeled "Christlam." It had a "social auxiliary" called "Guardians of Sperms."

Once again, he tried to find a religious outlet for his celebrity and his need. His financial state challenged his notions of manhood. As a Black Southern-born man Eldridge defined himself by economic independence, property rights, and being the head of his family. His political radicalism was an espousal of those ideological notions of what maleness represented as well as his foray into being an entrepreneur. Eldridge was in an angry push to make money to assert his manliness. In the end, he would be reduced to a scheme and a bad hustle, in marketing his infamous codpiece pants as something independently owned and produced by him. Visually the pants were all about the penis or "the dick." It was both a bad joke and a bad ploy. No pun intended—it asserted Black manhood. In selling and adverting those pants it was as though Eldridge had taken liberties with one of Richard Pryor's jokes when a White person asks why Black men stand on the corner holding their crotches. And Pryor's punch line answer, paraphrased, was "he's checking to see if it is still all there cause that's the only thing a nigger owns." Eldridge fully exhibited Pryor's joke. It sadly reduced him in desperation to a misogynistic caricature. White evangelicals would denounce him.

Although being an evangelical did not reward him financially as he hoped, Eldridge was not finished in his search to wed his dreams of building a stronger Black community with religion. He joined the Latter-Day Saints (LDS) in a continued search for a religious community that could be an alternative to the shortcomings of the liberal political state. He also hoped it would afford him some financial reward as he wrapped himself in the American flag as a reborn patriot.[53] His membership followed a consistent pattern; the LDS were well-organized, hierarchically male priests, and mystical, similar to Roman Catholics, the BPP, and the NOI. Eldridge was baptized into the LDS Church in 1983, just five years after the church began ordaining Black men to its priesthood.[54] He would make one last gambit to reach for power in the upper echelons of national politics by running for the US Senate in the California Republican primaries in 1986. He would receive a short run of publicity for his foray into elected politics, but that would be all.

Eldridge never found the correct formula for building a strong Black community within the bounds of a faith. His faiths had been Catholic, Islam, Marxist, American evangelical, and Mormon and they all disappointed him.

Perhaps the problem was how he assessed Black communities. He had tried to make a diverse and highly democratic community too uniform. He, perhaps, worried too much about the community's so-called brokenness and did not see the joys and strengths of the community that actually existed. When Eldridge died in 1998 at the young age of sixty-two, he was a man still in search of a faith that would aid him in building an ideal Black community. Former BPP chair Bobby Seale was forgiving of Eldridge's excesses in his brief eulogy of him.

As our information minister in the early years of the Black Panther Party, ELDRIDGE CLEAVER was a one-of-a-kind charismatic revolutionary who understood the politics of the human-liberation struggle. Party members called him "Papa" or "the Rage!" Fresh out of prison, he became a literary giant with his book *Soul on Ice*. Eldridge put his heart, mind and soul into the 1960s movement, but in the early '80s, I read that he said the party should have never existed. He tried to contact me, but I refused to speak with him. One day his ex-wife Kathleen called me to say Eldridge wanted to go on the lecture circuit with me and he wouldn't denounce our history. I figured he needed the money; and I remembered when he had money after *Soul on Ice*, he just handed it to me to organize things. We had become very close friends since we started lecturing together. A lot of people said negative things about Eldridge's being a born-again Christian and registered Republican; but I knew him beyond that, they didn't. Even as a Republican, he denounced Gingrich's Contract with America, throwing it across the stage. Sent the crowd wild. Like in the early years, he would do wild things, like challenging Ronald Reagan to a duel in the streets. He knew how to grab the imagination of the people! And that's just one of the many reasons I truly respected him.[55]

When I heard the news of his death, it stopped me and I thought about my own search for freedoms within Black community in which I lived and served. What were my own liberation dreams? I especially thought this after rewatching one of the last public interviews before his death in 1998 with Henry Louis Gates Jr. Gates did not spend any time querying him about his faith; I wish he would have. Eldridge's inner struggles and storying may have yielded more understanding as to what drove him into a social justice movement as transformed prisoner who became a fighter for freedom. Closing that interview, Gates asked:

> Will history judge you and your contemporaries from the '60s—Karenga, Rap, Stokely, Angela, the whole gang, Julian Bond—favorably, do you think?
>
> CLEAVER: I think they will. I think they will give us Fs where we deserve them and they'll give us As where we deserve them and they're going to give Huey P. Newton, Bobby Seale and Eldridge Cleaver an A plus.[56]

Eldridge should receive an A plus for his epic storying. In another set of posthumous, clipped-together interviews, Eldridge told Gates that he wished he could have been simply a writer.[57] He left enough paper. What we learned was that he was reflective and driven by an inner search for a personal and collective Black liberation, a utopian one. However contradictory, and yes demonic at times he was, he gets an A for storying himself into history as an infamous and complex character.

# Conclusion:

# We have been believers in a New Jerusalem

What is common to Ethel Waters, Mary Lou Williams, Muhammad Ali, and Eldridge Cleaver and to me are faith stories. These stories of faith are bound by individual opacity in a democratic political culture. These faith stories include both self-autonomy and the search for collective political power. This self-fashioning is part and parcel of the ethics of identity. Identity politics (a term too often used to disparage) are born of the personal struggle to care for one's self and political struggle of a community one is born into or voluntarily joins because of personal or political wrestles. These faith stories reflect how these individuals sought self-care, love, and dignity, as well as societal respect and civic freedoms. Faith stories are quilted. Quilts threaded with race, social class, sexualities and religion. No one is a flattened character, a purely one-dimensional person. These individual's faiths, whether religious or secular, are inextricably woven into political and personal struggles. They were found in the nineteenth-century American cultural mores that Alexis de Tocqueville witnessed and fumbled describing. This is the reason that culture critic Albert Murray in 1970 described Black Americans as "The Omni-Americans."

> *The Omni-Americans* is based in large measure on the assumption that since the negative aspects of black experience are constantly being overpublicized

(and to little purpose except to obscure the positive), justice to U.S. Negroes, not only as American citizens but also as the fascinating human beings that they so obviously are, is best served by suggesting some of the affirmative implications of their history and culture. After all, someone must at least begin to try to do justice to what U.S. Negroes like about being black and to what they like about being *Americans*. Otherwise justice can hardly be done to the incontestable fact that not only do they choose to live rather than commit suicide, but that, poverty and injustice notwithstanding, far from simply struggling in despair, they live with gusto and a sense of elegance that is always downright enviable.[1]

That gusto and elegance I argue are found in the joyful paradoxes of these faith stories.

Believers do not always have false consciousness. What they are looking for is an alternative epistemology, an alternative way of knowing and imagining the world anew. Faith storying is a reinvention of the world through divine empowerment. Storying through faith is both an assertion of individuality and a way of addressing struggles for a more just democracy. Storying is what the philosopher Kwame Anthony Appiah reflects upon regarding the ethics of identity.[2] Identity politics is born out of the struggle to care for one's self, and the political struggle to care for one's community.

Too frequently we have relegated persons to their roles without considering the context of their faith journeys, as though the ongoing and never-ending struggle for democratic freedoms is not shaped as much by faiths, conflict of faiths, and inner struggles as it is by education, social relations, and political activity. Perhaps it is time to stop looking at what is occurring around person unilaterally as though one set of things define a person's journey. Most folk have a consciousness, not a false one, but a consciousness shaped like the patches of a quilt—what the anthropologist Claude Lévi-Strauss called "bricolage."[3] It is uneven, but it is not false. Some parts are truer than others. That is the genius of storying.

"We Have Been Believers" by Margret Walker was published in 1942 in her volume of poetry titled *For My People*. In this award-winning volume, she depicts voicing and sonic punctuations of Black-inflected preaching. Those rhythms were so much of Walker's life, as they were my own. She grew up a child of a United Methodist preacher in New Orleans. Throughout the collection of poems, especially in "We Have Been Believers," she dramatically captures the difficult search and spiritual longing of Black Americans to transcendently escape the uneven hand dealt to them. Though sympathetic, Walker's poem is a critique of Black folk's religiosities. The poem in the end sees Black religiosity as being errant and delusional. She, like her writing compatriot Richard Wright, saw Black faith as an opiate and no substitute for political engagement. Walker followed Wright's lead in his notable book *12 Million Black Voices*, which also examined the ways Black folk engaged questions of faith as politically irrelevant. In the last two stanzas, she wrote:

Where are our gods that they leave us asleep? Surely the priests and the preachers and the powers will hear. Surely now that our hands are empty and our hearts too full to pray they will understand. Surely the sires of the people will send us a sign.

We have been believers believing in our burdens and our demigods too long. Now the needy no longer weep and pray; the long-suffering arise, and our fists bleed against the bars with a strange insistency.[4]

In fact, both Walker and Wright underestimated how Black Americans thought about their own faith struggles. Walker, influenced by Wright, missed Black opacity.[5] She, like Wright, adapted a form of Enlightenment modernism—the eighteenth-century set of mostly French ideas which viewed one particular way of thinking or reasoning as being exclusively true of all human beings.

It is unfortunate that Walker, the daughter of a Methodist minister, reduced the complexity of Black faith language to simply a false consciousness.[6] However, ordinary Black folk felt no need to speak in the language of an enlightened modernist. Adapting modernism would not make Black folk any more cosmopolitan or wiser on the subject of their own oppression, sufferings, or desires to be free. And it would not make them any more engaged in political fights for freedom. Instead, their peculiar agency and determined freedom to pursue their varied faith journeys had a much more powerful impact on their own political formation and that impact extended to foment political and social change in the United States and around the globe.

The philosopher Charles Taylor's masterfully takes us through a maze of philosophical musings in his book *The Sources of the Self*. Unfortunately, its valorization of European philosophical tradition and the eighteenth-century Enlightenment is exclusive and myopic. How could one talk about development of the self without discussing the Transatlantic Slave Trade or Native Removal as being central to the modern predicament throughout the Americas? These histories are at the center of modern self, the jagged self, the jazz self, and the storied self. However, his philosophical approach is on to something as he attempts to uncover the inner self. He's right when he writes that we all approach life via some type of inner frameworks.

> People may see their identity as defined partly by some moral or spiritual commitment, say as a Catholic, or an anarchist. Or they may define it in part by the nation or tradition they belong to, as an Armenian, say, or a Quebecois. What they are saying by this is not just that they are strongly attached to this spiritual view or background; rather it is that this provides the frame within which they can determine where they stand on questions of what is good, or worthwhile, or admirable, or of value. Put counterfactually, they are saying that were they to lose this commitment or identification, they would be at sea, as it were; they would not know anymore, for an important range of questions, what the significance was for them.[7]

I concur with Taylor's use of framework, whether it is as a collective group or an individual. As human beings, we are always trying to make sense and reinvent ourselves.[8] That is the essence of storying.

Black American frameworks have always been subject to much public discussion influenced by social sciences. These frameworks have been viewed too often as delusional and pathological from the empirical lens of social science.[9] However, faith storying was always more central to identity and life direction than the "objective investigators" seemed to suggest.

Historian Judith Weisenfeld in her most recent book *New World-a-Coming: Black Religion and Racial Identity during the Great Migration* captures this complexity as Black folk created new ways to name their own spiritual journeys or what Taylor calls frameworks. She eschews the reductive sociological labels that once were heaped on Black faith traditions by scholars. Weisenfeld specifically uses the term "religio-racial identity" to move beyond the reductive sociological descriptors that limited Black self-definitions of their own realities.[10] Black religious movements such as the NOI provided their own theological alternatives to define their communities, including what blackness meant, as free subjects within their own self-determining faith communities. In the words of Muhammad Ali, "I am free to be what I want to be."

Weisenfeld's book superbly documents the ways that autonomous claims to community supersede race. These same types of self-autonomous claims also held true for individuals. Being a Black Catholic, Muslim, Mormon, or Evangelical conflicted with some of the orthodox claims of those traditions even as Blacks maintained the hierarchical orthodoxies set along the lines of gender and sexuality. Later, greater demands for personal and democratic freedoms urged Black believers and nonbelievers alike to question any and all type of racially or sexually proscribed guardianship on their faiths.

What continues to strike me about these faith storifiers is how democratic they were. Whether they joined hierarchal religious organizations like the Roman Catholic Church or the Nation of Islam or more loose associations like the non-denominational Graham Crusade, each of these people brought with them democratic urgency in their public performances and personal struggles alike. Their storying gave expression to their right to exist on their own terms.

Black faiths, if anything, were born out of a marketplace of faiths that can be traced to a long heritage of West African pluralism. These storied tales of self-autonomy were also rooted in the marketplace of Black democratic thinking about faiths that dated back to American slavery. They stemmed from debates within and around Black Protestantism. These internecine arguments in point of fact could never be won in terms of whose truths were imperial or eternal. The more significant truth was that they democratically asserted an understanding that all Black women and men had the right to live and to express their various faiths, even in the case of the more clandestine ones. The logic of these faiths was that all women and men needed no justification to participate in their own governance.

These interior journeys are illustrative of Black American life generally. Whether Black people were guided by spiritual quests or self-realized journeys toward nonbelief, freedom to live with dignity as an individual and as a community was paramount. Historian Robin D. G. Kelley was correct to search the utopian ambitions of Black radical imagining in his book *Freedom Dreams*.[11] Yet he missed how faiths, not just radical ones, provided daily succor to endure and wage struggle. Faiths imaginatively permit inner visions that rise above social prohibitions. While social theorists are important in understanding societal structures, equally important are the inspired hopes born of out of faiths. The four subjects in this book all faced structural inequalities. They each suffered what is perennial to all of us—dissatisfaction, fear, insecurity, jealousy, and loneliness. In the words of Cornel West, riffing off the philosopher Soren Kierkegaard, dread, our deepest anxieties regarding our nonexistence or death. Yet, faith along with talent help them to manage their dreadful circumstances and make meaning for their lives and others.

So, this brings me back around to thinking about my own interiority. I grew up a Christian and have lived as a Christian in a cosmopolitan world of Blackness, what many scholars termed a Black Diaspora. Crisscrossing the Atlantic Oceans there are all kinds of competing faiths, though forms of Black

Protestantism have been dominant in the United States. Religious pluralism has always been inherent to Black communities. This reading of these storied individuals is in fact a testimony to that history. For me religious faith has been a good, though I recognize this is not true for everyone. I long gave up demanding that others share my faith in some uniform and domineering fashion. Faith is not imperialism, though sovereigns of one kind or another have sought to capture and legislate it. Using legalities and armies to enforce faith is no faith at all.

Black Americans have been democratically exemplary as persons of faiths. The history of Black American freedom struggles, perhaps, has seeded us this strength. We have operated, even if we have not completely understood it formally, a freedom to story ourselves around faiths. The framers of the US Constitution could not have imagined that it would be descendants of American slaves who in practice understood that a marketplace of faiths was and is necessary for civic freedoms to live. If there is such a thing as what John Dewey once called a common faith, it is this: the diversity of Black voices debating and storying to reinvent and live more holistically side by side with those who contest whatever faith practice they follow.[12] What is common to us is not one faith, but the protection of the right to express our faith stories freely.

Imperialistic forces often use faith to whip and brutalize. This is the dialectic that makes all faiths institutionally dangerous. Yet, I am reminded that the faiths that Black Americans have exhibited are a social good. The self-autonomy found in these four journeys, which includes their heterodoxies, as well orthodoxies, challenges us to scrutinize faith stories more carefully as inner histories. Faith for individuals is always a form of opacity. It is also one of the keys in playing the chords of democratic freedoms.[13]

A subtext of this book is a common ecumenism, not ones found in formal theological dogma or American civil religion, but one lived. This type of ecumenism should not be confused with the ideologically crafted understanding of an American Judeo-Christian tradition. A variety of thinkers from Protestant theologian Reinhold Niebuhr to conservative activist William Buckley, Jr. to the writer Will Herberg over a twenty-four-year period—1930 and 1954—shaped the notion that the Judeo-Christian ideal as central to American exceptionalism. They believed that the United States was inoculated from the Communist atheism because it was God-fearing.[14] Ideologically it presumed that religious faith made Americans more tolerant of each other and more open to people who held different faiths. This ideology was at its best mythic. The notion that the United States was a Judeo-Christian country was cheap wall paper. It attempted to hide the multiple inequities of an economy fueled by racial and gendered disparities.[15] In fact, each of these persons understood the realities of being American and criticized it publicly. None of them or their communities were completely tolerant. Their communities preached a narrow insistence that their way was correct and true. Yet in their actual lives they exhibited a broadness outside the dominion of clerics and politicians. Their tolerance came from the recognition of what it meant to be a put upon and put down people. They recognized their own self-freedoms and that of others. And this is the social good we must uphold.

These interior histories are also important sources for studying democracy in Black.[16] Each person examined here tried to live caring lives, however, inconsistent they might have been. Through their faiths, they fostered care. They organize power, charities, and aspirations. These faith storifiers attempted to expand their humanity by holding onto their own self-dreams and dreams of a collective future.

These histories of the self should give us pause. How will others one day read our own storied foibles and strengths, failures and successes religiously or otherwise? That answer lies well into the human future, if there is one. What I know for certain now is that a democracy that protect our right to faiths keeps hope alive for all of us.

# NOTES

## Introduction

1 Margaret Walker, "We Have Been Believers," *Internet Poetry Archive*, http://www. ibiblio.org/ipa/poems/walker/we_have_been_believers.php

2 Robert Orsi, *The Madonna of 115th Street: Faith and Community In Italian Harlem, 1880-1950* (New Haven: Yale University Press, 2002), 150.

3 Vincent Wimbush, *Bible and African Americans: A Brief History* (Philadelphia: Fortress Press, 2003); Allen Dwight Callahan, *The Talking Book: African Americans and the Bible* (New Haven: Yale University Press, 2008); Diane Proctor Reeder, *What the Word Be: Why Black English is the King's (James)* (Detroit: Written Images, 2014).

4 Guide to Religious Content in Slave Narratives Compiled by Marcella Grendler, Andrew Leiter, and Jill Sexton, http://docsouth.unc.edu/neh/religiouscontent.html

5 Theodore Parker, *The American Scholar*, edited by George Willis Cooke (Boston: American Unitarian Association, 1907), 44.

6 Clifton Herman Johnson, editor and introduction by Albert Raboteau, *God Struck Me Dead: Voices of Ex-Slaves* (Cleveland, OH: Pilgrim Press, 1969).

7 Kevin Young, *The Grey Album: On the Blackness of Blackness* (Minneapolis: Graywolf Press, 2012), 17–19.

8 Howard Thurman, *Deep River and The Negro Spiritual Speaks of Life and Death* (Richmond, Indiana; Friends United Press, 1975), 18.

9 W. E. B. DuBois, *Souls of Black Folk*, Chapter 14.

10 Thurman, *Deep River*, 62.

11 Ibid., 63.

12 Ibid., 65.

13 Margaret Walker, "For My People," *Poetry Foundation*, http://www.poetryfoundation. org/poetrymagazine/poem/11053

14 On narrative use of the Black Southern migration see Farah Jasmine Griffin, *"Who Set You Flowin'?": The African-American Migration Narrative* (New York: Oxford University Press, 1995).

15 See Milton Sernett, *Bound for the Promise Land: African American Religion and the Great Migration* (Durham: Duke University Press, 1997).

**16** On the making of the album see Aaron Cohen, *Aretha Franklin's Amazing Grace* (New York, NY: Continuum, 2011).

**17** "William Hebert Brewster Sr. (1897-1987)," in the *Tennessee Encyclopedia of History and Culture*, http://tennesseeencyclopedia.net/entry.php?rec=132

**18** Aretha Franklin, How I Got Over Lyrics, MetroLyrics, http://www.metrolyrics.com/how-i-got-over-lyrics-aretha-franklin.html#ixzz3yNuEoDrw

**19** Édouard Glissant, *Poetics of Relation*, translated by Betsy Wing (Ann Arbor: University of Michigan Press, 1997), 189.

**20** Glissant, *Poetics of* Relation, 190.

**21** Ibid., 191.

**22** Ibid., 192.

**23** Ibid., 194.

**24** Curtis J. Evans, *The Burden of Black Religion* (New York: Oxford University Press, 2008); Edward E. Curtis IV and Danielle Brune Sigler, eds., *The New Black Gods: Arthur Huff Fauset and the Study of African American Religions* (Bloomington: Indiana University Press, 2009).

**25** Robert Lipsyte, "Clay Discusses his Future, Liston and Black Muslims," *New York Times*, February 27, 1964, https://www.nytimes.com/books/98/10/25/specials/ali-future.html

**26** Nancy Tatom Ammerman, *Sacred Stories, Spiritual Tribes: Finding Religion in Everyday Life* (New York: Oxford University Press, 2014), 9.

**27** Charles Marsh, *God's Long Summer: Stories of Faith and Civil Rights* (Princeton, NJ: Princeton University Press, 1998).

**28** Reading Kirby Moss's, *The Color of Class: Poor Whites and the Paradox of Privilege* (Philadelphia: University of Pennsylvania Press, 2003) served as an impetus to put myself into this story. Moss investigation of poor Whites forced him to reflect on his own journey.

**29** Elizabeth Alexander, *The Black Interior* (Minneapolis: Graywolf Press, 2004), x–xi.

**30** Alexander, *The Black* Interior, 5.

**31** Anthony Pinn, *Varieties of African American Religious Experience* (Minneapolis: Augsburg-Fortress, 1998), 3.

**32** Martin E. Marty, *Righteous Empire: The Protestant Experience in America* (New York: Dial Press, 1970).

**33** See Ross Posnock, *Color & Culture: Black Writers and the Making of the Modern Intellectual* (Cambridge, MA: Harvard University Press, 1998).

**34** James Baldwin, *The Fire Next Time* (New York: Bantam Doubleday Dell Publishing Group, 1963), 16–20.

# Chapter 1

1 On the creation of Aunt Jemima see M. M. Manning, *Slave in a Box: The Strange Career of Aunt Jemima* (Charlottesville, VA: University of Virginia Press, 1998).

2 "Irritating Women," *The New York Times Magazine*, May 16, 1999, http://www. nytimes.com/1999/05/16/magazine/irritating-women.html?pagewanted=all

3 Darlene Clark Hine, "Rape and the Inner Lives of Black Women in the Middle West," *Signs* 14, no. 4 (Summer 1989), 915.

4 Hine, "Rape and the Inner Lives of Black Women in the Middle West," 916. Hine observes: "White's allusion to 'resultant suspicion' speaks implicitly to one important reason why so much of the inner life of Black women remains hidden. Indeed, the concepts of 'secrets' and 'dissemblance,' as I employ them, hint at those issues that Black women believed better left unknown, unwritten, unspoken except in whispered tones. Their alarm, their fear, or their Victorian sense of modesty implies that those who broke the silence provided grist for detractors' mills and, even more ominously, tore the protective cloaks from their inner selves. Undoubtedly, these fears and suspicions contribute to the absence of sophisticated historical discussion of the impact of rape (or threat of rape) and incidences of domestic violence on the shape of Black women's experiences."

5 Marla Frederick, *Between Sundays: Black Women and Everyday Struggles of Faith* (Berkeley, CA: University of Carolina Press, 2003).

6 Frederick, *Between Sundays*, 14–18.

7 Quoted in James F. Wilson, *Bulldykes, Pansies, and Chocolate Babies: Performance, Race and Sexuality in the Harlem Renaissance* (City University of New York PhD Dissertation 2000), 1.

8 Lerone A. Martin, *Preaching on Wax: The Phonograph and the Shaping of Modern African American Religion* (New York: New York University Press, 2014).

9 Michael S. Weaver, "Makers and Redeemers: The Theatricality of the Black Church," *Black American Literature Forum* 25, no. 1 (1991), St. Louis University: 53–61.

10 Wallace Best, *Passionately Human, No Less Divine: Religion and Culture in Black Chicago, 1915-1952* (Princeton: Princeton University Press, 2007); Chad Heap, *Slumming: Sexual and Racial Encounters in American Nightlife 1885-1945* (Chicago: University of Chicago Press, 2010); Kevin J. Mumford, *Interzones: Black/White Sex Districts in Chicago and New York in the Early Twentieth Century* (New York: Columbia University Press, 1997).

11 On Billy Graham's politics of decency see: Steven P. Miller, *Billy Graham and the Rise of the Republican South* (Philadelphia: University of Pennsylvania Press, 2007), 3.

12 James Earl Massey, "African Americans and Evangelicalism," *Fuller Magazine*, https:// fullermag.fuller.edu/african-americans-evangelicalism/

13  Donald Bogle, *Heat Wave: The Life and Career of Ethel Waters* (New York: HarperCollins, 2011), 461.

14  Patricia Caldwell, *The Puritan Conversion Narrative: The Beginnings of American Expression* (Cambridge: Cambridge University Press, 1983).

15  Harvey Breit, "Talk With Ethel Waters," *New York Times*, March 18, 1951, BR 12.

16  Breit, "Talk With Ethel Waters."

17  Ibid.

18  Ethel Waters with Charles Samuels, *His Eye Is on the Sparrow: An Autobiography* (New York: Da Capo Press, 1992), 1.

19  On Black women's labor struggles and resistance, see: Tera Hunter's *To 'Joy My Freedom: Southern Black Women's Lives and Labor After the Civil War* (Cambridge: Harvard University Press, 1998); Jacqueline Jones, *Labor of Love, Labor of Sorrow: Black Women, Work, and the Family From Slavery to Freedom.*

20  Waters, *His Eye Is on the Sparrow*, 7–19.

21  Ibid.; Jacqueline Jones, *Labor of Love, Labor of Sorrow*, edited by Jacqueline Jones (Basic Books, 2009). ProQuest Ebook Central. Created from ku on 2017-05-06 12:40:26.

22  Ibid., 8.

23  Ibid., 19.

24  Bogle, *Heat Wave*, 7.

25  Waters, *His Eye Is on the Sparrow*, 9.

26  Ibid., 20–21.

27  St. Peter Claver Roman Catholic Church Records Finding Aid by Annalise Berini and Steven Duckworth, http://dla.library.upenn.edu/dla/pacscl/ead.pdf?id=PACSCL_TUSCRC_TUBlockson002; Rachel Moloshok, "Memories of St. Peter Claver Church," *Pennsylvania Legacies* 15, no. 2 (2015): 3–5. Academic OneFile. Web. April 17, 2016, http://go.galegroup.com.www2.lib.ku.edu/ps/i.do?id=GALE%7CA428275925&v=2;

Steven A. Marquez, "St. Peter Claver Closed? Parish The Thought," *Philadelphia Inquirer*, June 27, 1986, http://articles.philly.com/1986-06-27/news/26045377_1_catholic-parishes-holy-communion-unique-church; Faith Charlton, "Black Catholics in Philadelphia and The Journal," February 24, 2011, Philadelphia Archdiocesan Historical Research Center, http://www.pahrc.net/black-catholics-in-philadelphia-and-the-journal/; Lou Baldwin, "Black Catholics' Traditional Home in the Archdiocese to Close," October 9, 2014, CatholicPhilly.com, http://catholicphilly.com/2014/10/news/local-news/black-catholics-traditional-home-in-archdiocese-to-close/

28  Cyprian Davis, *The History of Black Catholics in the United States* (New York: Crossroads Publishing, 1990), 23.

29  Pierre Suau, "St. Peter Claver," The Catholic Encyclopedia, vol. 11 (New York: Robert Appleton Company, 1911), April 2, 2013, http://www.newadvent.org/cathen/11763a.htm

**30** H. Richard Niebuhr, *The Social Sources of Denominationalism* (New York: Holt, 1929).

**31** Waters, *His Eye Is on the Sparrow*, 36.

**32** Ibid., 47.

**33** Ibid., 48.

**34** Ibid., 50.

**35** Ibid., 51–52.

**36** Frederick, *Between Sundays*, 64.

**37** Henry Hewes, "Ethel Waters and A Hymn: An Actress Talks About the Song She Sings," *New York Times*, April 30, 1950, X2.

**38** Bogle, *Heat Wave*, 95.

**39** Waters, *His Eye Is on the Sparrow*, 58–64.

**40** Ibid., 66.

**41** Ibid., 82.

**42** Ibid., 110.

**43** Ibid., 115.

**44** Ibid., 117.

**45** Angela Davis, *Blues Legacies and Black Feminism: Gertrude "Ma" Rainey, Bessie Smith, and Billie Holiday* (New York: Vintage Books, 1999).

**46** Bogle, *Heat Wave*, 12.

**47** I am indebted to Shannon J. Miller's, "African-American Lesbian Identity Management and Identity Development in the Context of Family and Community," *Journal Of Homosexuality* 58, no. 4 (April 2011): 547–63. LGBT Life with Full Text, EBSCOhost (accessed May 11, 2016) on regarding African American communal sense of "don't ask, don't tell" approach to questions of lesbian identities. Historically, I would argue this pattern is rooted in a broader context of racial subordination.

**48** See Kevin J. Mumford, *Interzones: Black/White Sex Districts in Chicago and New York in the Early Twentieth Century*; Chad Heap, *Slumming: Sexual and Racial Encounters in American Nightlife, 1885-1940*; *Hidden from History: Re-claiming the Gay and Lesbian Past,* ed. Martin Bauml Duberman, Martha Vicinus, and George Chauncey Jr. (New York: New American Library, 1989)

**49** See Elaine Tyler May, *Homeward Bound: American Families in the Cold War Era* (New York: Basic Books, 1988)

**50** There is a rich body of literature on Christianity and sexuality that I have been influenced by beginning with John Boswell's breakthrough book *Christianity, Social Tolerance and Homosexuality: Gay People in Western Europe from the Beginning of* *the Christian Era to the Fourteenth Century* (Chicago: University of Chicago Press, 1980); Peter Brown, *The Body and Society: Men, Women, and Sexual Renunciation in Early Christianity* (New York: Columbia University Press, 2008); Steven Ozment, *When Fathers Ruled: Family Life in Reformation Europe* (Cambridge, MA: Harvard University Press, 1985); Kyle Harper, *From Shame to Sin: The Christian Transformation of Sexual Morality in Late Antiquity* (Cambridge, MA: Harvard University Press, 2016).

51   See the brilliant elucidation of the fetish in Sylvester Johnson's *African American Religions, 1500-2000: Colonialism, Democracy, and Freedom* (New York: Cambridge University Press, 2015).

52   Waters, *His Eye Is on the Sparrow*, 78–79.

53   Earl Wilson, "Ethel Waters—Torch Singer to Dramatic Actress," *New York Post*, December 6, 1940, NP.

54   Ira Berlin, *Suppertime*, Metro, http://www.metrolyrics.com/suppertime-lyrics-irving-berlin.html

55   Bogle, *Heat Wave*, 227.

56   Ibid.

57   Waters, *His Eye Is on the Sparrow*, 93.

58   Earl Wilson, "Ethel Waters—Torch Sing to Dramatic Actress," *NYP*.

59   On sacred space see Meredith B. McGuire, *Lived Religion: Faith and Practice in Everyday Life* (New York: Oxford University Press, 2008), 225–26; Ammerman, *Sacred Stories, Spiritual Tribes*, 76.

60   History of the Carmel of St. Therese of the Child of Jesus, http://www.carmelite-nuns.com/Allentown_Carmel_History.htm

61   Sherrie Tucker, "When Subjects Don't Come Out," in *Queer Episodes: In Music and Modern Identity*, edited by Sophie Fuller and Lloyd Whitesell (Urbana: University of Illinois Press, 2002), 304.

62   Waters, *His Eye Is on the Sparrow*, 48.

63   Ibid., 52.

64   Whitney R. Cross, *The Burnt-over District: The Social and Intellectual History of Enthusiastic Religion in Western New York, 1800–1850* (Ithaca: Cornell University Press, 1981).

65   Harry S. Stout, *The Divine Dramatist: George Whitefield and the Rise of Modern Evangelicalism* (Grand Rapids: Eerdmans Publishing, 1991), xviii.

66   Stout, *The Divine* Dramatist, xix.

67 Oral History 203, Ethel Waters's Oral Interview with Lois Fern, Baton Rouge, Louisiana, October 1970, Billy Graham Oral History Project, Wheaton College, Wheaton Illinois

68 Michael Emerson and Christian Smith, *Divided by Faith: Evangelical Religion and the Problem of Race in America* (New York: Oxford University Press, 2001).

69 Waters, Ethel & Graham, Billy, 1918– & Howard, Floretta 1952, Ethel Waters letters, approximately 1952-1977, https://trove.nla.gov.au/work/227883326

70 Martin Luther King, Jr., My Pilgrimage Towards Nonviolence, September 1, 1958, http://kingencyclopedia.stanford.edu/encyclopedia/documentsentry/my_pilgrimage_to_nonviolence1.1.html

71 Gary Dorrien, *The New Abolitionist: W.E.B. DuBois and Black Social Gospel* (New Haven, CT: Yale University Press, 2015).

72 Jonathan Reider, *The Word of the Lord is Upon Me: The Righteous Performance of Martin Luther King, Jr.* (Cambridge, MA: Harvard University Press, 2008).

73 See letter from Grady Wilson to King in 1958, https://kinginstitute.stanford.edu/king-papers/documents/grady-wilson

74 Prayer Pilgrimage for Freedom, http://kingencyclopedia.stanford.edu/encyclopedia/encyclopedia/enc_prayer_pilgrimage_for_freedom_1957/

75 Martin Luther King, Jr., Give Us the Ballot Address at the Prayer Pilgrimage for Freedom, May 17, 1957, Washington DC, http://kingencyclopedia.stanford.edu/encyclopedia/documentsentry/doc_give_us_the_ballot_address_at_the_prayer_pilgrimage_for_freedom/index.html

76 Grant Wacker, *America's Pastor: Billy Graham and the Shaping of a Nation* (Cambridge, MA: Harvard University Press, 2014).

# Chapter 2

1 C. Gerald Fraser, "Ethel Waters is Dead at 80," *New York Times* (1923–Current File), September 2, 1977, http://search.proquest.com.www2.lib.ku.edu/docview/123149126?accountid=14556

2 Martin Bandyke, "Nothing Beats Brick-and-Mortars Record Stores," *Ann Arbor News*, August 30, 2009, http://www.annarbor.com/entertainment/nothing-beats-brick-and-mortar-record-stores/

3 Sherrie Tucker, "Big Ears: Listening for Gender in Jazz Studies," *Current Musicology* Numbers 71–73 (Spring 2001–Spring 2002): 71–73.

4  Sam Hamilton-Poore, exploring the spirituality of John Coltrane, writes "There is ample evidence to suggest that, with *A Love Supreme*, Coltrane was purposefully building a musical bridge across which ordinary listeners might pass as pilgrims to experience and celebrate the holy. Furthermore, the spirituality of *A Love Supreme* has been reflected upon, written about, interpreted and reinterpreted by musicians, critics, musicologists, sociologists, and people on the street more than perhaps any other jazz recording of the 1960s. There is, in other words, an abundance of material from generations of listeners that is interdisciplinary, diverse, and cross-generational." "John Coltrane's *A Love Supreme*, Yesterday and Today: Breaking Boundaries, Testing Limits, *Spiritus* 13, no. 2 (2013): 189."

5  Nichole T. Rustin, "'Mary Lou Williams Plays Like A Man!' Gender, Genius and Difference in Black Music Discourse," *The South Atlantic Quarterly* 104, no. 3 (July 2005): 442–62.

6  Theodore E. Buehrer, ed., *Mary's Ideas: Mary Lou Williams's Development as a Big Band Leader* (Madison, Wisconsin: Music of the United States of America (MUSA), vol. 25: A-R Editions, 2013).

7  Langston Hughes, *Selected Poems of Langston Hughes* (New York: Vintage Books, 1974), 83 (Fair Use).

8  Lil Hardin Armstrong, "Satchmo and Me," *American Music* 25, no. 1 (2007): 106–18; Chris Albertson, *Lil Hardin Armstrong Memphis Music Hall of Fame*, http://memphismusichalloffame.com/inductee/lilhardinarmstrong/

9  See Linda Dahl, *Morning Glory*, 204–05; Tammy Kernodle, *Soul on Soul*, 137.

10  1 Kgs 19 KJV.

11  Duke Ellington, *Music is My Mistress* (New York: DeCapo Paperback, 1976).

12  Thomas Forbes, "The Social History of the Caul," *Yale Journal of Biology and Medicine* 25, no. 6 (June 1953): 495–508.

13  Walter C. Rucker, "Caul," *The Encyclopedia of African American History*, vol. I, edited by Leslie Alexander and Walter C. Rucker (Santa Barbara, CA: ABC-CLIO Publisher, 2010), 176

14  Rich, Carroll Y. "Born with the Veil: Black Folklore in Louisiana," *The Journal of American Folklore* 89, no. 353 (1976): 328–31.

15  "Veil, in African American Culture," *International Encyclopedia of the Social Sciences*, 2008. Encyclopedia.com, August 10, 2016, http://www.encyclopedia.com/doc/1G2-3045302893.html

16  Farah Jasmine Griffin, *Harlem Nocturne: Women Artists & Progressive Politics During World War II* (New York: Basic Civitas, 2013), 183.

17  Griffin, *Harlem Nocturne*, 164.

18  Henry H. Mitchell, *Black Belief: Folk Beliefs of Black Americans and West Africans* (New York: Harper and Row, 1975).

19 Keith Thomas, *Religion and the Decline of Magic: Popular Beliefs in Sixteenth and Seventeenth Century England* (New York: Oxford University Press, 1971).

20 Thurman, *Deep River.*

21 Davis, *The History of Black Catholics in the United States*, 243–47.

22 Cecilia A. Moore, Cyprian Davis and Wallace Best, "Keeping Harlem Catholic: African-American Catholics and Harlem," *American Catholic Studies* 114, no. 3 (September 2003): 3–21.

23 Stephen J. Ochs, *Desegregating the Altar: The Josephites and the Struggle for Black Priests, 1871–1960* (Baton Rouge: Louisiana State University Press, 1993).

24 See Matthew J. Cressler, *Authentically Black and Truly Catholic: The Rise of Black Catholicism in the Great Migration* (New York: New York University Press, 2017).

25 Albert J. Raboteau, "Black Catholics and Afro-Religious History: Autobiographic Reflections," *U.S. Catholic Historian* 5, no. 1, The Black Catholic Experience (1986): 119–27.

26 Moore, Davis, and Best, "Keeping Harlem Catholic," 10.

27 Kernodle, *Soul on Soul*, 178–79.

28 Iain Anderson, *This is Our Music: Free Jazz, the Sixties and American Culture* (Philadelphia: University of Pennsylvania Press, 2007), 17–24; also see Penny Von Eschen, *Satchmo Blows Up the World: Jazz Ambassadors Play the Cold War* (Cambridge, MA: Harvard University Press, 2006).

29 Dahl, *Morning Glory*, 228–29.

30 Anderson, *This is Our Music*, 78–80.

31 On Holiday see Farah Jasmine Griffin, *If You Can't Be Free, Be a Mystery: In Search of Billie Holiday* (New York: Ballantine, 2002).

32 Dahl, *Morning Glory,* 302.

33 Thomas Merton, *The Living Bread* (New York: Farrar, Strauss & Cudahy, 1956), 6.

34 Merton, *The Living Bread*, 25.

35 Peter A. Dorsey, *Sacred Estrangement: The Rhetoric of Conversion in Modern American Autobiography* (University Park, Pennsylvania: Pennsylvania State University Press, 1993), 25.

36 Kernodle, *Soul on Soul*, 180.

37 Dahl, *Morning Glory*, 247.

38 On the concept of natal alienation see Orlando Patterson's *Slavery and Social Death: A Comparative Study* (Cambridge, MA: Harvard University Press, 1982).

**39** Gayle Murchison, "Mary Lou Williams's Hymn *Black Christ of the Andes (St. Martin de Porres):* Vatican II, Civil Rights, and Jazz as Sacred Music," *The Music Quarterly* 86, no. 4 (Winter 2002): 591–629.

**40** See Martha Biondi's *To Stand and Fight: The Struggle for Civil Rights in Postwar New York* (Cambridge, MA: Harvard University Press, 2003).

**41** Cited in Murchison, "Mary Lou Williams's Hymn *Black Christ of the Andes,*" 597.

**42** Ibid., 603.

**43** Cited in Father Peter O'Brien, SJ Liner Notes, *Black Christ of the Andes*, Mary Lou Williams, Smithsonian Folkway Recordings, CD, 40816, 2004.

**44** Ibid.

**45** Kernodle, *Soul on Soul*, 180.

**46** Father Peter O'Brien, SJ Liner Notes, *Black Christ of the Andes*, Mary.

**47** "The Prayerful One," *Time*, February 21, 1964.

**48** David Jackson, "Jazz is Her Religion: Mary Lou Williams," *Black Creation Annual 1974*, 50.

# Chapter 3

**1** Geoffrey C. Ward, *Unforgivable Blackness: The Rise and Fall of Jack Johnson* (New York: Vintage, 2006); Theresa Runstedler, *Jack Johnson, Rebel Sojourner: Boxing in the Shadow of the Global Color Line* (Berkeley, CA: University of California Press, 2012).

**2** On Haley's *The Autobiography of Malcolm* see Manning Marable's *Malcolm X: A Life of Reinvention* (New York: Viking Press, 2011).

**3** See Jacob Dorman, *Chosen People: The Rise of American Black Israelite Religions* (New York: Oxford University Press, 2013); Judith Weisenfeld, *New World A-Coming: Black Religion and Racial Identity During the Great Migration* (New York: New York University Press, 2017).

**4** Richard Wright, *Black Boy* (New York: Harper Collins Publisher, 1991).

**5** See Ula Yvette Taylor's marvelous *The Promise of Patriarchy: Women and the Nation of Islam* (Chapel Hill: University of North Carolina Press, 2017), 15.

**6** Stephen R. Haynes, *Noah's Curse: The Biblical Justification of American Slavery* (New York: Oxford University Press, 2002); David M. Goldenberg, *The Curse of Ham: Race and Slavery in Early Judaism, Christianity and Islam* (Princeton, NJ: Princeton University Press, 2003).

7  Randy Roberts and Johnny Smith, *Blood Brothers: The Fatal Friendship between Muhammad Ali and Malcolm X* (New York: Basic Books, 2016), 102.

8  George C. Wright, *Life Behind the Veil: Blacks in Louisville, Kentucky 1865–1930* (Baton Rouge: Louisiana State University Press, 1985).

9  P. J. Hutchison, "From Bad Buck to White Hope: Journalism and Sonny Liston, 1958–1965," *Journal of Sports Media* 10, no. 1 (2015): 119–37. Retrieved from https://search-proquest-com.www2.lib.ku.edu/docview/1664814034?accountid=14556

10  Jonathan Eig, *Ali: A Life* (Boston and New York: Houghton, Mifflin, Harcourt, 2017), 87.

11  Roberts and Smith, *Blood Brothers*, 145–50.

12  Muhammad Ali with Richard Durham, *The Greatest: My Own Story* (New York: Random House, 1975).

13  Quoted in Thomas Hauser's *Muhammad Ali: His Life and Times* (New York: Touchstone, 1991), 95.

14  Ibid., 102.

15  Alan H. Levy, *Floyd Patterson: A Boxer and a Gentleman* (Jefferson, NC: McFarland & Company, 2008); W. K. Stratton, *Floyd Patterson: The Fighting Life of Boxing's Invisible Champion* (Boston: Houghton Mifflin Harcourt, 2012); Floyd Patterson with Milton Gross, *Victory Over Myself* (New York: Bernard Geis Associates, 1962).

16  Floyd Patterson and Milton Gross, "I Want to Destroy Clay," *Sports Illustrated*, October 19, 1964, 43.

17  Patterson and Gross, "I Want to Destroy Clay."

18  Annette Gordon-Reed, "The Persuader," *The New Yorker*, June 13, 2011, http://www.newyorker.com/magazine/2011/06/13/the-persuader-annette-gordon-reed;

On Josiah Henson, *The Life of Josiah Henson, Formerly a Slave, Now an Inhabitant of Canada, as Narrated by Himself*, http://docsouth.unc.edu/neh/henson49/summary.html

19  William Jeremiah Moses, *Black Messiahs and Uncle Toms: Social and Literary Manipulations of a Religious Myth* (University Park, Pennsylvania: The Pennsylvania University Press, 1992).

20  Hauser, *Muhammad Ali*, 162–63.

21  On Fard see: Karl Evanzz, *The Messenger: The Rise and Fall of Elijah Muhammad* (New York: Pantheon Books, 1999); Claude Andrew Clegg III, *An Original Man: The Life and Times of Elijah Muhammad* (New York: St. Martin's 1997). On the NOI's sacred history see Weisenfeld, *New World A-Coming*, 56–73.

22  Bill Russell with Tex Maule, "I Am Not Worried About Ali," *Sports Illustrated*, June 19, 1967, 18–21.

**23** Hauser, *Muhammad Ali*, 144–45.

**24** William Safire, "On Language: Family Values," *New York Times*, September 6, 1992, http://www.nytimes.com/1992/09/06/magazine/on-language-family-values.html

**25** Taylor, *The Promise of Patriarchy*, Chapter 7.

**26** Elijah Muhammad, *Message to a Blackman* (Atlanta, GA: Elijah Muhammad Propagation Society, Reprint of 1965 edition, 1997).

**27** Taylor, *The Promise of Patriarchy*, Chapter 5.

**28** Anthea Butler, *Women in the Church of God in Christ: Making a Sanctified World* (Chapel Hill: University of North Carolina Press, 2007).

**29** E. Franklin Frazier, *Negro Family in the United States* (Chicago: University of Chicago Press, 1966).

**30** One of the controversial discussions is regarding the relationship between Malcolm X and Betty Shabazz in Manning Marable's *Malcolm X: A Life of Reinvention*.

**31** Sonsyrea Tate, *Little X: Growing Up in the Nation of Islam* (San Francisco: Harpers, 1997).

**32** Kwame Anthony Appiah, *The Ethics of Identity* (Princeton, NJ: Princeton University Press, 2005), 163.

# Chapter 4

**1** T. D. Allman, "The Rebirth of Eldridge Cleaver," *The New York Times*, January 16, 1977, 197.

**2** Bio on T. D. Allman University of North Florida, http://www.unf.edu/uploadedFiles/aa/coas/english/td%20allman%20bio.pdf

**3** Stevie Wonder, "Jesus People," *Innervisions* (Motown Records, 1973) (Fair Use).

**4** Molly Worthen, "John Stott, C.S. Lewis, and J.R.R. Tolkien: Why American Evangelicals Love the British," *Religion and Politics*, May 1, 2012, http://religionandpolitics.org/2012/05/01/john-stott-c-s-lewis-j-r-r-tolkien-why-american-evangelicals-love-the-british/

**5** Kathleen N. Cleaver, "Why Eldridge Cleaver Has Come Home," *Los Angeles Times*, Opinion Page, December 1975 (Los Angeles, CA: Times-Mirror, 1975), 2.

**6** Bayard Rustin file on Eldridge Cleaver, including Cleaver's comments concerning Fidel Castro, Africa, and Cuban Blacks, Cleaver's reasons for return to the United States., life in France, activities of Bayard Rustin for Cleaver defense and Rustin's support of Cleaver, and People of the State of California v. Cleaver, 1975–77, http://congressional.proquest.com/histvault?q=001581-001-0368

7   Khalil G. Muhammad, *Condemnation of Blackness: Race, Crime, and Making of Modern Urban America* (Cambridge, MA: Harvard University Press, 2011).

8   Austin Reed, *The Life and Adventures of Haunted Convict*, edited by Caleb Smith (New York: Modern Library; Reprint edition, 2017).

9   John A. Oliver, *Eldridge Cleaver: Reborn* (Plainfield, NJ: Logos International, 1977), 49.

10   L. Eldridge Cleaver to Beverly Axelrod, May 26, 1965, Bancroft Library University of California, Berkeley; Kathleen Sullivan, "Beverly Axelrod—Attorney for Black Panthers," *San Francisco Chronicle*, June 21, 2002, http://www.sfgate.com/bayarea/article/Beverly-Axelrod-attorney-to-Black-Panthers-2805883.php

11   Ibid., Cleaver to Axelrod.

12   Ibid., Cleaver to Axelrod.

13   Leigh Schmidt, *Restless Souls: The Making of American Spirituality* (Berkeley: University of California Press, Second Edition, 2012).

14   Roger A. Berger, "Soul on Ice," in *The Oxford Companion to African American Literature*, edited by William Andrews and Francis Smith Foster (New York: Oxford University Press, 1997), 157.

15   Michael Taylor, "Ex-Black Panther Eldridge Cleaver/ 'Soul on Ice' author, voice of black resistance was 62," *San Francisco Chronicle*, May 2, 1998, http://www.sfgate.com/news/article/Ex-Black-Panther-Eldridge-Cleaver-Dies-Soul-on-3007656.php

16   Eldridge Cleaver, *Soul on Ice* (New York: Dell Publishing, 1991), 23.

17   Stephen "Donny" Donaldson, "A Million Jockers, Punks, and Queens," in *Prison Masculinities*, edited by Donald F. Sabo, Terry Allen Kupers, and Willie James London (Philadelphia, PA: Temple University Press, 2001), 118.

18   Tommy J. Curry, *The Man-Not: Race, Class, Genre, and the Dilemmas of Black Manhood* (Philadelphia: Temple University Press, 2017), Chapter 2.

19   Cleaver, *Soul on Ice*, 128–29.

20   Donaldson, "A Million Jockers, Punks, and Queens," 119–20.

21   Cleaver, *Soul on Ice*, 135.

22   On the question of masculinity in *Soul on Ice* see Douglas Taylor, "Three Lean Cats in Hall of Mirrors: James Baldwin, Norman Mailer and Eldridge Cleaver on Race and Masculinity," *Texas Studies in Literature and Language* 52, no. 1 (Spring 2010): http://muse.jhu.edu/article/374955

23   Curry, *The Man-Not*, 85–86.

24  Cleaver, *Soul on Ice*, 34.

25  Ibid., 35.

26  Ibid., 82.

27  Ibid., 110.

28  Ibid., 120

29  Ibid., 120–21.

30  Ibid., 50.

31  Ibid.

32  Ibid., 51.

33  Ibid.

34  Ibid., 55–56.

35  See Jane Naomi Iwamura's *Virtual Orientalism: Asian Religion and American Popular Culture* (New York: Oxford University Press, 2011), 41–52.

36  Cleaver, *Soul on Ice*, 52.

37  Ibid., 53.

38  Ibid., 54.

39  Jeffrey M. Burns, "No Longer Emerging: Ramparts Magazine and the Catholic Laity, 1962–1968," *U.S. Catholic Historian* 9, no. 3 (June 1990): 321–33.

40  Eldridge Cleaver, *Post-Prison Writings and Speeches*, edited and with Introduction by Robert Scheer (New York: Vintage Books, 1968), 204.

41  Cleaver, *Post-Prison Writings and Speeches*, 74.

42  Ibid., 76.

43  Henry Louis Gates Jr., "Eldridge Cleaver On Ice," *Transition* 75/76 1997; Research Library, 29.

44  Ibid., 40.

45  Angela Dillard, *Guess Who's Coming to Dinner Now? Multicultural Conservatism in America* (New York: New York University, 2001), Chapter 1.

46  Cleaver, *Post-Prison Writings and Speeches*, 95–107.

47  Ashley Lavelle, "From 'Soul on Ice' to 'Soul for Hire'? The Political Transformation of Black Panther Eldridge Cleaver," *Race & Class*, Institute of Race Relations 54, no. 2 (2012): 55–74.

48  Eldridge Cleaver, *Soul on Fire* (Waco, Texas: Word Books, 1978), 37–38.

49  Elaine Brown, *Taste of Power* (New York, Knopf-Doubleday, 1992), 225; Kathleen Cleaver is silent on this aspect of her marriage. See Somini Sengupta, "Memories of a Proper Girl Who Was A Panther," *New York Times*, June 17, 2000, http://www.nytimes.com/2000/06/17/books/memories-of-a-proper-girl-who-was-a-panther.html

50  Cleaver, *Soul on Fire*, 211.

51  Randy Frame, "Whatever Happened to Eldridge Cleaver," *Christianity Today* 28 (April 20, 1984): 38.

52  See Diane Winston and John M. Giggie, eds, *Faith in the Market: Religion and Rise of Urban Commercial Culture* (New Brunswick, NJ: Rutgers University Press, 2002).

53  *Eldridge Cleaver: Brigham Young University Speech*. Educational Video Group, 1981 (accessed February 21, 2017).

54  Newell G. Bringhurst, "Eldridge Cleaver's Passage through Mormonism," *Journal of Mormon History* 28, no. 1 (Spring 2002), 83.

55  Bobby Seale, "Eulogy," *Time* 151, no. 18 (May 11, 1998).

56  Henry Louis Gates Jr., "Interview with Eldridge Cleaver," *Two Nations of Black America Frontline*, http://www.pbs.org/wgbh/pages/frontline/shows/race/interviews/ecleaver.html

57  *Leaving Cleaver: Henry Louis Gates, Jr., Remembers Eldridge Cleaver* by Darren Duarte; June Cross; Henry Louis Gates, Jr.; Eldridge Cleaver; Kathleen Cleaver; Michael Simollari; Earl R Johnson; Films for the Humanities & Sciences (Firm); Films Media Group.; Public Broadcasting Service (United States); WGBH Educational Foundation (New York, NY: Film Media Group, 2011).

# Conclusion

1  Albert Murray, *The Omni-Americans: New Perspectives on the Black Experience and American Culture* (New York: Outerbridge and Dienstrfrey, 1970).

2  Appiah, *The Ethics of Identity*.

3  Claude Lévi-Strauss, *The Savage Mind* (Chicago: University of Chicago Press, 1996).

4  Margaret Walker, "We Have Been Believers," *Poetry: A Magazine of Verse* LIII, no. VI (March 1939), https://www.poetryfoundation.org/poetrymagazine/browse?contentId=22290

5  Wallace Best, *Passionately Human, No Less Divine: Religion and Culture in Black Chicago, 1915-1952* (Princeton: Princeton University Press, 2006).

6　Randal Maurice Jelks, "Masculinity, Modernism, and Religion: A Consideration of Benjamin Elijah Mays and Richard Wright," *Women, Gender, and Families of Color* 2, no. 1 (Spring 2014): 57–78.

7　Charles Taylor, *Sources of the Self: The Making of Modern Identity* (Cambridge, MA: Harvard University Press, 1989), 27.

8　Taylor, *Sources of the Self*, 16–18.

9　Daryl Michael Scott, *Pity and Contempt: Social Policy and the Image of the Damage Black Psyche, 1880-1996* (Chapel Hill: University of North Carolina Press, 1997).

10　Judith Weisenfeld, *New World-a-Coming*, see her Introductory Chapter.

11　Robin D. G. Kelley, *Freedom Dreams: The Black Radical Imagination* (Boston: Beacon Press, 2003).

12　John Dewey, *A Common Faith* (New Haven: Yale University Press, 2nd edition, 2013).

13　Orlando Patterson, *Freedom: Freedom in the Making of Western Culture Volume I* (New York: Basic Books, 1992).

14　Jason W. Stevens, *God-Fearing: A Spiritual History of the Cold War* (Cambridge, MA: Harvard University Press, 2010).

15　Will Herberg, *Protestant, Catholic, Jew: An Essay in American Religious Sociology* (Garden City, NY: Doubleday, 1955); Mia Sara Bruch, "Religious Pluralism and the Judeo-Christian Tradition," Franklel Institute for Advanced Judaic Studies, University of Michigan Volume 2012, http://hdl.handle.net/2027/spo.11879367.2012.008; Dianne Kirby, "Anglo-American Relations and the Religious Cold War," *Journal of Transatlantic Studies* 10, no. 9 (2012): 167–81; Andrew Preston, "Introduction: The Religious Cold War," in *Religion and the Cold War*, edited by Philip Muehlenbeck (Nashville: Vanderbilt University Press, 2012); and James C. Wallace, "A Religious Cold War?: The Cold War and Religion," *Journal of Cold War Studies* 15, no. 3 (Summer 2013): 162–80; K. Healan Gaston, " The Cold War Romance of Religious Authenticity: Will Herberg, William Buckley, Jr. and the Rise of the New Right," *Journal of American History* 99, no. 4 (March 2013): 1133–58.

16　Eddie Glaude, Jr., *Democracy in Black: How Race Still Enslaves the American Soul* (New York: Crown, 2016).

# SELECT BIBLIOGRAPHY

## Published Primary Sources

### Muhammad Ali

Muhammad Ali with Richard Durham, *The Greatest: My Own Story* (New York: Random House, 1975).
Jack Olsen, *Black Is Best: The Riddle of Cassius Clay* (New York: Putnam, 1967).
Bill Russell with Tex Maule, "I Am Not Worried About Ali," *Sports Illustrated* June 19, 1967, 18–21.

### Eldridge Cleaver

Eldridge Cleaver, *Post-Prison Writing and Speeches*, edited by Robert Scheer (New York: Random House, 1969).
Eldridge Cleaver, *Soul on Ice* (New York: Dell Publishing, 1991).
Eldridge Cleaver Papers Bancroft Library Special Collection, University of California Berkeley.
Eldridge Cleaver Papers 1959–1981 Cushing Library Texas A&M University.
Eldridge Cleaver Papers *Brigham Young University Speech*. Educational Video Group, 1981. Accessed February 21, 2017.
Kathleen Neal Cleaver, "On Eldridge Cleaver," *Ramparts*, Volume 8 June 1969 (San Francisco, CA), 4, 6, 8, 10–11.
*Leaving Cleaver: Henry Louis Gates, Jr., Remembers Eldridge Cleaver* by Darren Duarte; June Cross; Henry Louis Gates, Jr.; Eldridge Cleaver; Kathleen Cleaver; Michael Simollari; Earl R Johnson; Films for the Humanities & Sciences (Firm); Films Media Group.; Public Broadcasting Service (U.S.); WGBH Educational Foundation (New York, NY: Film Media Group, 2011).

### Ethel Waters

Harvey Breit, "Talk With Ethel Waters," *New York Times* March 18, 1951, BR 12.
C. Gerald Fraser, "Ethel Waters Is Dead at 80." *New York Times* (1923–Current File), September 2, 1977.

Henry Hewes, "Ethel Waters and A Hymn: An Actress Talks About the Song She Sings," *New York Times* April 30, 1950, X2.

Oral History 203, Ethel Waters' Oral Interview with Lois Fern, Baton Rouge, Louisiana, October, 1970, Billy Graham Oral History Project, Wheaton College, Wheaton Illinois.

Ethel Waters, *To Me It's Wonderful* introduction by Eugenia Price and Joyce Blackburn (New York: Harper & Row, 1972).

Ethel Waters and Billy Graham, 1918– & Howard, Floretta 1952, Ethel Waters letters, approximately 1952–1977 https://trove.nla.gov.au/work/227883326.

Ethel Waters R Billy Graham Archives, Wheaton College, and Wheaton, Illinois, BGCA Mss 13 Box 2 F. 24.

Ethel Waters with Charles Samuels, *His Eye Is on the Sparrow: An Autobiography* (New York: Da Capo Press, 1992).

Earl Wilson, "Ethel Waters—Torch Singer to Dramatic Actress," *New York Post*. December 6, 1940, NP.

## Mary Lou Williams

Peter F. O'Brien, "Jazz for the Soul," Liner Notes, *Black Christ of the Andes*.

Mary Lou Williams Paper, Institue of Jazz Studies, Rutgers-Newark.

Mary Lou Williams, "In Her Own Words," *Melody Maker* https://ratical.org/MaryLouWilliams/MMiview1954.html.

# Other Published Sources

Stephen "Donny" Donaldson, "A Million Jockers, Punks, and Queens," in *Prison Masculinities*, edited by Donald F. Sabo, Terry Allen Kupers, and Willie James London (Philadelphia, PA: Temple University Press, 2001).

Josiah Henson, *The Life of Josiah Henson, Formerly a Slave, Now an Inhabitant of Canada, as Narrated by Himself*, http://docsouth.unc.edu/neh/henson49/summary.html.

George Jackson, *Soledad Brother: The Prison Letters of George Jackson* (Chicago: Lawrence Hill, 1994).

Martin Luther King, Jr. Prayer Pilgrimage for Freedom https://kinginstitute.stanford.edu/encyclopedia/prayer-pilgrimage-freedom.

Martin Luther King, Jr., My Pilgrimage Towards Nonviolence September 1, 1958 http://kingencyclopedia.stanford.edu/encyclopedia/documentsentry/my_pilgrimage_to_nonviolence1.1.html.

Floyd Patterson with Milton Gross, *Victory Over Myself* (New York: Bernard Geis Associates, 1962).

Floyd Patterson and Milton Gross, "I Want to Destroy Clay," *Sports Illustrated*, October 19, 1964, 43.

Sonsyrea Tate, *Little X: Growing Up in the Nation of Islam* (San Francisco: Harpers, 1997).

# Secondary Writings

Elizabeth Alexander, *The Black Interior* (Minneapolis: Graywolf Press, 2004).

Nancy Tatom Ammerman, *Sacred Stories: Finding Religion in Everyday Life* (New York: Oxford University Press, 2014).

Iain Anderson, *This Is Our Music: Free Jazz, the Sixties and American Culture* (Philadelphia: University of Pennsylvania Press, 2007).

William Andrews and Francis Smith Foster, *The Oxford Companion to African American Literature* (New York: Oxford University Press, 1997).

Kwame Anthony Appiah, *The Ethics of Identity* (Princeton: Princeton University Press, 2005).

James Baldwin, *The Fire Next Time* (New York: Bantam Doubleday Dell Publishing Group, 1963).

Lou Baldwin, "Black Catholics' Traditional Home in the Archdiocese to Close," October 9, 2014 CatholicPhilly.com http://catholicphilly.com/2014/10/news/local-news/black-catholics-traditional-home-in-archdiocese-to-close/.

Martin Bauml Duberman, Martha Vicinus, and George Chauncey Jr., eds., *Hidden from History: Re- claiming the Gay and Lesbian Past* (New York: New American Library, 1989).

Wallace Best, *Passionately Human, No Less Divine: Religion and Culture in Black Chicago, 1915–1952* (Princeton: Princeton University Press, 2007).

Donald Bogle, *Heat Wave: The Life and Career of Ethel Waters* (New York: HarperCollins, 2011).

John Boswell, *Christianity, Social Tolerance and Homosexuality: Gay People in Western Europe from the Beginning of the Christian Era to the Fourteenth Century* (Chicago: University of Chicago Press, 1980).

Newell G. Bringhurst, "Eldridge Cleaver's Passage Through Mormonism," *Journal of Mormon History* 28: 1 (Spring 2002), 83.

Elaine Brown, *Taste of Power* (New York, Knopf-Doubleday, 1992), 225.

Peter Brown, *The Body and Society: Men, Women, and Sexual Renunciation in Early Christianity* (New York: Columbia University Press, 2008).

Mia Sara Bruch, "Religious Pluralism and the Judeo-Christian Tradition," Franklel Institute for Advanced Judaic Studies, University of Michigan Volume 2012: http://hdl.handle.net/2027/spo.11879367.2012.008.

Theodore E Buehrer, ed., *Mary's Ideas: Mary Lou Williams's Development as a Big Band Leader* (Madison, WI: Music of the United States of America (MUSA) vol. 25: A-R Editions, 2013).

Jeffrey M. Burns, "No Longer Emerging: Ramparts Magazine and the Catholic Laity, 1962–1968." *U.S. Catholic Historian*, vol. 9, no. 3 (June 1990), 321–33.

Anthea Butler, *Women in the Church of God in Christ: Making a Sanctified World* (Chapel Hill: University of North Carolina Press, 2007).

Patricia Caldwell, *The Puritan Conversion Narrative: The Beginnings of American Expression* (Cambridge: Cambridge University Press, 1983).

Allen Dwight Callahan, *The Talking Book: African Americans and the Bible* (New Haven: Yale University Press, 2008).

Faith Charlton, "Black Catholics in Philadelphia and The Journal," February 24, 2011 Philadelphia Archdiocesan Historical Research Center http://www.pahrc.net/black-catholics-in-philadelphia-and-the-journal/.

Clegg III, Claude Andrew, *An Original Man: The Life and Times of Elijah Muhammad* (New York: St. Martin's 1997).

Aaron Cohen, *Aretha Franklin's Amazing Grace* (New York, NY: Continuum, 2011).

Tommy J. Curry, *The Man-Not: Race, Class, Genre, and the Dilemmas of Black Manhood* (Philadelphia: Temple University Press, 2017).

Edward E. Curtis IV and Danielle Brune Sigler, eds., *The New Black Gods: Arthur Huff Fauset and the Study of African American Religions* (Bloomington: Indiana University Press, 2009).

Whitney R. Cross, *The Burnt-over District: The Social and Intellectual History of Enthusiastic Religion in Western New York, 1800–1850* (Ithaca: Cornell University Press, 1981).

Linda Dahl, *Morning Glory: A Biography of Mary Lou Williams* (New York: Pantheon Books, 1999).

Cyprian Davis, *The History of Black Catholics in the United States* (New York: Crossroads Publishing, 1990).

Angela Davis, *Blues Legacies and Black Feminism: Gertrude "Ma" Rainey, Bessie Smith, and Billie Holiday* (New York: Vintage Books, 1999).

John Dewey, *A Common Faith* (New Haven: Yale University Press, 2nd ed., 2013).

Angela Dillard, *Guess Who's Coming to Dinner Now? Multicultural Conservatism in America* (New York: New York University, 2001).

Jacob Dorman, *Chosen People: The Rise of American Black Israelite Religions* (New York: Oxford University Press, 2013).

Gary Dorrien, *The New Abolitionist: W.E.B. DuBois and Black Social Gospel* (New Haven, CT: Yale University Press, 2015).

Peter A. Dorsey, *Sacred Estrangement: The Rhetoric of Conversion in Modern American Autobiography* (University Park, PA: Pennsylvania State University Press, 1993).

W. E. B. DuBois, Introduction by Shawn Leigh Alexander, *Souls of Black Folks: Essay and Sketches* (Amherst: University of Massachusetts Press, 2018).

Curtis J. Evans, *The Burden of Black Religion* (New York: Oxford University Press, 2008).

Karl Evanzz, *The Messenger: The Rise and Fall of Elijah Muhammad* (New York: Pantheon Books, 1999).

Michael Emerson and Christian Smith, *Divided by Faith: Evangelical Religion and the Problem of Race in America* (New York: Oxford University Press, 2001).

Thomas Forbes, "The Social History of the Caul," *Yale Journal of Biology and Medicine* 25: 6 (June 1953): 495–508.

Marla Frederick, *Between Sundays: Black Women and Everyday Struggles of Faith* (Berkeley, CA: University of Carolina Press, 2003).

K. Healan Gaston, " The Cold War Romance of Religious Authenticity: Will Herberg, William Buckley, Jr. and the Rise of the New Right," *Journal of American History* 99: 4, March 1, 2013: 1133–58.

Eddie Glaude, Jr, *Democracy in Black: How Race Still Enslaves the American Soul* (New York: Crown, 2016).

Édouard Glissant, translated by Betsy Wing, *Poetics of Relation* (Ann Arbor: University of Michigan Press, 1997).

David M. Goldenberg, *The Curse of Ham: Race and Slavery in Early Judaism, Christianity and Islam* (Princeton, NJ: Princeton University Press, 2003).

Farah Jasmine Griffin, *"Who Set You Flowin'?": The African-American Migration Narrative* (New York: Oxford University Press, 1995).

Farah Jasmine Griffin, *Harlem Nocturne: Women Artists & Progressive Politics During World War II* (New York: Basic Civitas, 2013).

Farah Jasmine Griffin, *If You Can't Be Free, Be a Mystery: In Search of Billie Holiday* (New York: Ballantine, 2002).

Sam Hamilton-Poore, "John Coltrane's *A Love Supreme*, Yesterday and Today: Breaking Boundaries, Testing Limits," *Spiritus* 13: 2 (2013): 189.

Kyle Harper, *From Shame to Sin: The Christian Transformation of Sexual Morality in Late Antiquity* (Cambridge, MA: Harvard University Press, 2016).

Stephen R. Haynes, *Noah's Curse: The Biblical Justification of American Slavery* (New York: Oxford University Press, 2002).

Thomas Hauser's *Muhammad Ali: His Life and Times* (New York: Touchstone, 1991).

Chad Heap, *Slumming: Sexual and Racial Encounters in American Nightlife 1885–1945* (Chicago: University of Chicago Press, 2010).

Will Herberg, *Protestant, Catholic, Jew: An Essay in American Religious Sociology* (Garden City, NY: Doubleday, 1955).

Darlene Clark Hine, "Rape and the Inner Lives of Black Women in the Middle West," *Signs* 14: 4 (Summer 1989).

Langston Hughes, *Selected Poems of Langston Hughes* (New York: Vintage Books, 1974).

Tera Hunter *To 'Joy My Freedom: Southern Black Women's Lives and Labor After the Civil War* (Cambridge, MA: Harvard University Press, 1998).

Judy L. Isaken, "Veil, in African American Culture." *International Encyclopedia of the Social Sciences*. 2008. Encyclopedia.com. (August 10, 2016). http://www.encyclopedia.com/doc/1G2-3045302893.html.

Jane Naomi Iwamura's *Virtual Orientalism: Asian Religion and American Popular Culture* (New York: Oxford University Press, 2011).

Margo Jefferson, "Chameleon: Ethel Waters" in "Irritating Women," *The New York Times Magazine* May 16, 1999 http://www.nytimes.com/1999/05/16/magazine/irritating-women.html?pagewanted=all.

Clifton Herman Johnson, editor and introduction by Albert Raboteau, *God Struck Me Dead: Voices of Ex Slaves* (Cleveland, Ohio: Pilgrim Press, 1969).

Sylvester Johnson, *African American Religions, 1500–2000: Colonialism, Democracy, and Freedom* (New York: Cambridge University Press, 2015).

Jacqueline Jones, *Labor of Love, Labor of Sorrow: Black Women, Work, and the Family From Slavery to Freedom* (New York: Basic Books, 2nd ed., 2009).

Robin D. G. Kelley, *Freedom Dreams: The Black Radical Imagination* (Boston: Beacon Press, 2003).

Tammy Kernodle, *Soul on Soul: The Life and Music of Mary Lou Williams* (Boston: Northeastern University Press, 2004).

Dianne Kirby, "Anglo-American Relations and the Religious Cold War," *Journal of Transatlantic Studies* 10: 9 (2012): 167–81.

Ashley Lavelle, "From 'Soul on Ice' to 'Soul for Hire'? The Political Transformation of Black Panther Eldridge Cleaver," *Race & Class* Institute of Race Relations 54: 2: (2012): 55–74.

Claude Levi-Strauss, *The Savage Mind* (Chicago: University of Chicago Press, 1996).

Alan H. Levy, *Floyd Patterson: A Boxer and a Gentleman* (Jefferson, NC: McFarland & Company, 2008).

Meredith B. McGuire, *Lived Religion: Faith and Practice in Everyday Life* (New York: Oxford University Press, 2008).

M. M. Manning, *Slave in a Box: The Strange Career of Aunt Jemima* (Charlottesville, VA: Unsiversity of Virginia Press, 1998).

Manning Marable's *Malcolm X: A Life of Reinvention* (New York: Viking Press, 2011).

Charles Marsh, *God's Long Summer: Stories of Faith and Civil Rights* (Princeton, NJ: Princeton University Press, 1998).

Steven A. Marquez, "St. Peter Claver Closed? Parish The Thought," *Philadelphia Inquirer* June 27, 1986 http://articles.philly.com/1986-06-27/news/26045377_1_catholic-parishes-holy-communion-unique-church.

Lerone A. Martin, *Preaching on Wax: The Phonograph and the Shaping of Modern African American Religion* (New York: New York University Press, 2014).

Martin E. Marty, *Righteous Empire: The Protestant Experience in America* (New York: Dial Press, 1970).

James Earl Massey, "African Americans and Evangelicalism," *Fuller Magazine* https://fullermag.fuller.edu/african-americans-evangelicalism/.

Elaine Tyler May, *Homeward Bound: American Families in the Cold War Era* (New York: Basic Books, 1988).

Shannon J. Miller, "African-American Lesbian Identity Management and Identity Development in the Context of Family and Community," *Journal Of Homosexuality* 58: 4 (April 2011): 547–63.

Steven P. Miller, *Billy Graham and the Rise of the Republican South* (Philadelphia: University of Pennsylvania Press, 2007).

Steven P. Miller, *The Age of Evangelicalism: America's Born Again Years* (New York: Oxford University Press, 2016).

Henry H. Mitchell, *Black Belief: Folk Beliefs of Black Americans and West Africans* (New York: Harper and Row, 1975).

Rachel Moloshok, "Memories of St. Peter Claver Church," *Pennsylvania Legacies* 15: 2 (2015): 3–5.

Cecilia A. Moore, Cyprian Davis and Wallace Best, "Keeping Harlem Catholic: African-American Catholics and Harlem," *American Catholic Studies* 114: 3 (September 2003): 3–21.

William Jeremiah Moses, *Black Messiahs and Uncle Toms: Social and Literary Manipulations of a Religious Myth* (University Park, PA: The Pennsylvania University Press, 1992).

Kirby Moss, *The Color of Class: Poor Whites and the Paradox of Privilege* (Philadelphia: University of Pennsylvania Press, 2003).

Khalil G. Muhammad, *Condemnation of Blackness: Race, Crime, and Making of Modern Urban America* (Cambridge, MA: Harvard University Press, 2011).

Kevin J. Mumford, *Interzones: Black/White Sex Districts in Chicago and New York in the Early Twentieth Century* (New York: Columbia University Press, 1997).

Gayle Murchison, "Mary Lou Williams's Hymn *Black Christ of the Andes (St. Martin de Porres)*: Vatican II, Civil Rights, and Jazz as Sacred Music," *The Music Quarterly* 86: 4 (Winter, 2002).

Albert Murray, *The Omni-Americans: New Perspectives on the Black Experience and American Culture* (New York: Outerbridge and Dienstrfrey, 1970).

H. Richard Niebuhr, *The Social Sources of Denominationalism* (New York: Holt, 1929).

Stephen J. Ochs, *Desegregating the Altar: The Josephites and the Struggle for Black Priests, 1871–1960* (Baton Rouge: Louisiana State University Press, 1993).

John A. Oliver, *Eldridge Cleaver: Reborn* (Plainfield, NJ: Logos International, 1977).

Robert Orsi, *The Madonna of 115th Street: Faith and Community In Italian Harlem, 1880–1950* (New Haven: Yale University Press, 2002).

Theodore Parker, *The American Scholar*, edited by George Willis Cooke (American Unitarian Association, 1907).

Orlando Patterson, *Freedom: Freedom in the Making of Western Culture Volume I* (New York: Basic Books, 1992).

Anthony Pinn, *Varieties of African American Religious Experience* (Minneapolis: Augsburg-Fortress, 1998).

Ross Posnock, *Color & Culture: Black Writers and the Making of the Modern Intellectual* (Cambridge, MA: Harvard University Press, 1998).

Andrew Preston, "Introduction: The Religious Cold War," in Philip Muehlenbeck (ed.), *Religion and the Cold War: A Global Perspective* (Nashville: Vanderbilt University Press, 2012).

Albert J. Raboteau, "Black Catholics and Afro-Religious History: Autobiographic Reflections," *U.S. Catholic Historian* 5: 1, The Black Catholic Experience (1986): 119–27.

Austin Reed, *The Life and Adventures of Haunted Convict*, edited by Caleb Smith (New York: Modern Library; Reprint edition, 2017).

Diane Proctor Reeder, *What the Word Be: Why Black English Is the King's (James)* (Detroit: Written Images, 2014).

Jonathan Reider, *The Word of the Lord Is Upon Me: The Righteous Performance of Martin Luther King, Jr.* (Cambridge, MA: Harvard University Press, 2008).

Carroll Y. Rich, "Born with the Veil: Black Folklore in Louisiana," *The Journal of American Folklore* 89: 353 (1976): 328–31.

Randy Roberts and Johnny Smith, *Blood Brothers: The Fatal Friendship Between Muhammad Ali and Malcolm X* (New York: Basic Books, 2016).

Theresa Runstedler, *Jack Johnson, Rebel Sojourner: Boxing in the Shadow of the Global Color Line* (Berkeley, CA: University of California Press, 2012).

Nichole T. Rustin, "'Mary Lou Williams Plays Like A Man!' Gender, Genius and Difference in Black Music Discourse," *The South Atlantic Quarterly* 104: 3 (July 2005): 442–62.

Donald F. Sabo, Terry Allen Kupers, and Willie James London, eds., *Prison Masculinities* (Philadelphia, PA: Temple University Press, 2001).

William Safire, "On Language: Family Values," *New York Times* September 6, 1992 http://www.nytimes.com/1992/09/06/magazine/on-language-family-values.html.

Leigh Schmidt, *Restless Souls: The Making of American Spirituality* (Berkeley: University of California Press, 2nd ed., 2012).

Milton Sernett, *Bound for the Promise Land: African American Religion and the Great Migration* (Durham: Duke University Press, 1997).

Jason W. Stevens, *God-Fearing: A Spiritual History of the Cold War* (Cambridge, MA: Harvard University Press, 2010).

Harry S. Stout, *The Divine Dramatist: George Whitefield and the Rise of Modern Evangelicalism* (Grand Rapids: Eerdmans Publishing, 1991).

W. K. Stratton, *Floyd Patterson: The Fighting Life of Boxing's Invisible Champion* (Boston: Houghton Mifflin Harcourt, 2012).

Pierre Suau, "St. Peter Claver," *The Catholic Encyclopedia*, Vol. 11. New York: Robert Appleton Company, 1911. April 2, 2013 http://www.newadvent.org/cathen/11763a.htm.

Charles Taylor, *Sources of the Self: The Making of Modern Identity* (Cambridge, MA: Harvard University Press, 1989).

Douglas Taylor, "Three Lean Cats in Hall of Mirrors: James Baldwin, Norman Mailer and Eldridge Cleaver on Race and Masculinity," *Texas Studies in Literature and Language* 52: 1, Spring 2010 http://muse.jhu.edu/article/374955.

Ula Yvette Taylor, *The Promise of Patriarchy: Women and the Nation of Islam* (Chapel Hill: University of North Carolina Press, 2017).

Keith Thomas, *Religion and the Decline of Magic: Popular Beliefs in Sixteenth and Seventeenth Century England* (New York: Oxford University Press, 1971).

Howard Thurman, *Deep River and The Negro Spiritual Speaks of Life and Death* (Richmond, IN: Friends United Press, 1975).

Sherrie Tucker, "When Subjects Don't Come Out," in *Queer Episodes: In Music and Modern Identity*, edited by Sophie Fuller and Lloyd Whitesell (Urbana: University of Illinois Press, 2002).

Sherrie Tucker, "Big Ears: Listening for Gender in Jazz Studies," *Current Musicology* Numbers 71–73 (Spring 2001–Spring 2002), 71–73.

Grant Wacker, *America's Pastor: Billy Graham and the Shaping of a Nation* (Cambridge, MA: Harvard University Press, 2014).

Margaret Walker, "For My People," *Poetry Foundation* http://www.poetryfoundation.org/poetrymagazine/poem/11053.

Geoffrey C. Ward, *Unforgivable Blackness: The Rise and Fall of Jack Johnson* (New York: Vintage, 2006).

Michael S. Weaver, "Makers and Redeemers: The Theatricality of the Black Church," *Black American Literature Forum* 25: 1 (1991) St. Louis University: 53–61.

Judith Weisenfeld, *New World A-Coming: Black Religion and Racial Identity During the Great Migration* (New York: New York University Press, 2017).

James F. Wilson, *Bulldykes, Pansies, and Chocolate Babies: Performance, Race and Sexuality in the Harlem Renaissance* (City University of New York Ph.D. Dissertation 2000).

Vincent Wimbush, *Bible and African Americans: A Brief History* (Philadelphia: Fortress Press, 2003).

Penny Von Eschen, *Satchmo Blows Up the World: Jazz Ambassadors Play the Cold War*, (Cambridge, MA: Harvard University Press, 2006).

George C. Wright, *Life Behind the Veil: Blacks in Louisville, Kentucky 1865–1930* (Baton Rouge: Louisiana State University Press, 1985).

Kevin Young, *The Grey Album: On the Blackness of Blackness* (Minneapolis: Graywolf Press, 2012).

# INDEX